Argyro Toumazou delivered her first speech at twelve when she graduated from elementary school. After success in secretarial studies, she followed a challenging career as a secretary/personal assistant. She enhanced her intellectual abilities by getting a degree in Law (Private), Athens University. At the beginning of her new career in the administrative/executive sector, she came face to face with a crude and complex reality. In her effort to mitigate the accruing hardships, she attended a motivation course with clinical psychologist Nicki Michael, finding her guidance and advice of great help.

Her past experience taught her that she could do much more with her life instead of letting time pass without better outcomes.

Currently she is a successful author in the book series Bird's Milk with the book *Develop your Power of Thought* and in the Polity Series with the book *Polity and Cyprus*. She published a book she translated from French under the title *Le Pouvoir Judiciaire*. She is also an aspiring coach in individual and political development.

To all readers aspiring for a successful mind control mindset.

Argyro Toumazou

MIND AND THOUGHT

Learning to Create Using Dynamic Thoughts

AUSTIN MACAULEY PUBLISHERS™

LONDON • CAMBRIDGE • NEW YORK • SHARJAH

A CIP catalogue record for this title is available from the British Library.

ISBN 9781787103443 (Paperback)
ISBN 9781787103450 (Hardback)
ISBN 9781787103467 (E-Book)

www.austinmacauley.com

First Published (2018)
Austin Macauley Publishers Ltd.
25 Canada Square
Canary Wharf
London
E14 5LQ

Acknowledgements

Ulrich H. Kiefer of Strasbourg Ortenau assisted me with the programme for the book format and the trimming of the photos appearing on my website.

Warning – Disclaimer

Argyro Toumazou

The ideal speaker for your next event

A few words of Motivation and Inspiration:

"Knowledge does not apply itself; we as individuals must make the application."
"By keeping the thought in the mind it will gradually take a tangible form."
"The only way to keep from going backward is to keep going forward."

To schedule Argyro to speak at your event:
Phone+ 357 99401728   Fax +357 22771728
www.glowcontrol.org

Introductory Note

It may be more of a legend that our mind is liable to development. To some it may come as a lifestyle norm, to others by way of necessity as a means to fulfil their ambitions, and to others as a simple propensity to curiosity. Besides, human beings have an inner tendency to antagonism expressed in all walks of activity. Once the human mind is capable of surging ahead, it may also run the risk of staying stunted or rolling backwards. Such trends are manifest and occur to individuals and societies. Classification may be subjective. Attitudes and predilections are abundant and varied.

Time, energy, standard of health, even commitments to our fellows often stand in our way of a better fulfilment of our aspirations. Striking the right balance and overcoming a variety of adversities is part of the game.

Finally, the choice is strictly personal. Even when we rely on expert advice, we do it with a sense of trust and hope for the best whilst conscious of possible limitations. Whatever the consideration, a better informed mind offers us the benefit of sharpening our eyes and wits and gives us a step ahead against the odds. In this game, the winners are on the positive side.

How to Use Your Power of Thought

From this moment you are beginning a new era in your life. You will realise that you have a great power and that your thoughts control your life. Things that are happening to you do not happen by mere chance or accident. You cause them to happen.

You are the keeper and the owner of an improbable mechanism of power, which can change and convert your life from the moment that you learn how to use it. You are going to learn the significant rules that control and manage your life. This is precisely the priceless value of this book.

It shows you how you have personal power and how to understand things that are happening to you and why they are happening!

Argyro Toumazou

Learn to create using your dynamic thoughts!

"Share this Book"

Your Power of Thought

Fifty Steps

Everyone needs to be reminded of the importance of becoming creative using their personal power, and everyone can come to realise that this power really exists. This book offers simple techniques. Mind control exercises that enable you to use your power in order to acquire whatever you want in your life: health, love, joy, harmony, wellbeing. Everything.

To place an order, visit **www.glowcontrol.org** or call **+357 99401728**

Table of Contents

1

Develop Your Power of Thought

We are living simultaneously in two worlds, not one: **First** is our internal world, our thoughts and feelings. **Second** is our external world. You are sitting in your room reading this book. You see the wall, the furniture, and other things.

In the internal world, though you are in your room, you may be thinking what is going to happen when you go out of your home, or you may be thinking something that happened to you in the past. That is, you can be, while you are in the external world, in your room, yet in your internal world you may be found in a different place completely. We always do this. That is, we live in two worlds at the same time.

Most of the time, our internal world is dominated by our external world. We always, in one way or another, react. When something goes well for us, we feel beautiful; but when something does not go well, we feel displeased, sad, angry, etc. However, there is no such a thing as sadness in the external world. Simply there are things happening that we interpret in our mind in a way that makes us feel displeased and sad.

> **"First you must find a suitable place for your bees, one sheltered from the wind, etc."**
> **Virgil, *Georgic. IV. 8***

The Quickest Traveller

The quickest traveller is no one else but our own mind. Be it our memory, our imagination or forethought, it works wonders for us. Nevertheless, as the demands grow, our mind may refuse to respond at different paces; for example, when we are in a hurry, or when we feel upset, it may get blocked for a while. After all, as far as this is occasional and on secondary matters, a transient lapse of recollection is not a particular source of anxiety.

What is best is to get as organised as possible so as to be able to retrieve our mental files without delay or inconvenience. Modern technology affords us many aids that enable us to enjoy a high degree of organisation. There seems to be no end to our organising demands. A good self-knowledge is indispensable in this regard. Knowing our reserves and limitations is a valuable guide to the accomplishment of our daily tasks. Having a reliable team and good networks is most valuable and a great privilege.

A good network, however, as well as a great privilege will never come out of its way to find us. We happen to live in a world of a most high complexity. This is not a new occurrence; what is new is that complexity gradually gets tenser around most of us. Our only outlet is to concentrate on the best possible organisation we can and to harmonise conflicting situations.

The speed of thought, being "mind in motion" depends entirely on the mechanism to which it is attached, as we read in Chapter 3. The hit or hits obtained, being either images or ideas, vary from an empirical point of view. This variation is due to a number of factors including age, learning, orientation, sentimental bend, interest, state of health and, essentially, our immediate priorities.

We usually enquire further in an issue relying on six faithful servants: who, what, where, when, why and how. These servants reveal to us all the information we need in every course of action or non-action. They are aids to our judgement about what is true or what is false on the one hand and on the other about what we must or must not do under the given circumstances and also disclose to us the extent of our freedom of action.

We are unequivocally part of nature and at the same time we are part of a community or network. Within these bounds formulating our external world we have our internal territory, our internal world. Our response to our external world seems to operate on the basis of two alternatives. At any given moment, we either create or react, as we see in Chapter 2. Our object in this book is to do our best to reinforce and safeguard the first alternative and eliminate as much as we can the second. In the pursuit of this objective, our freedom of action hangs invariably on our freedom of thought and on the influence we can exert on the aforesaid factors, each one viewed in its own ambit.

The mind is also capable of getting ideas or feelings from other individuals without the immediate interference of the senses in exceptional circumstances. Such passage is attributed to a state of mind called telepathy and occurs on rather rare occasions between persons of particular affinity or sharing a common concern. This mental process is instant and simultaneous.

2
Create – Don't React

Self-confidence does not exist in the external world; only in our thought, in our mind. The same applies to fear, unhappiness, happiness and so on. What we are going to learn in this book is not to react. With the mechanism of our mind we can learn how to create, using our dynamic thoughts. We are going to learn how to do everything in our internal world, without concerning ourselves about the external reality. We become creative by releasing our personal power. This power really exists.

The universe can work only with the materials that are given to it for each thing. One law in the universe governs all things. The same exactly happens with us. Through our power of thought we have access to the cause of each and every thing that is happening to us, both pleasant and unpleasant. We, and only we, have the option to create them. Our position in the world depends upon three conditions. We derive a right from two of these conditions, and the world bases its duty upon the third. This right and duty rest on the expression: "I exist for myself, the world exists for me, I exist for the world." What we are and who we are today is due to all the thoughts and ideas we have had since our childhood.

"What determines the experiences with which we meet in life? – Our predominant mental attitude."
Charles F. Haanel, *The Master Key System*

External Threats

Some people have been designed by nature to have a mild demeanour. They go about their lives in a well-composed and good-natured manner.

Others, not so gifted, look unstable in mood. As if configured by fortune or up-bringing, they often run their spirits out of control, though on the whole they regain their good self without inflicting a remainder of ill effect. Bringing their character to a better level requires considerable self-observation. Once they realise their predicament, they have at their disposal a way out. Unfortunately, easily irritated characters lack this kind of self-knowledge and determination. They blatantly enthral themselves to their explosive mood habit.

It is the third category, anyway, that comes to be of concern to us. Their pathological condition remains invariably sinister. They seem attached to a source of negative vibration. Assuming a vampire role, they emit an ill demeaning feeling of contempt terrorising their chosen victims whenever the latter cross their path. Without circumspection or shame they direct a penetrating current of panic at them in a conspicuous manner intending to harass and offend them.

By way of reaction one has no hesitation in returning a courteous response to a kind and affable person. A reciprocal respect and honour is most welcome. The same attitude does not apply in the second case. A more careful conduct is advisable. A considerable degree of self-control and patience is required every time we are called to overcome sudden blues. Seeking a quiet moment can work out a desirable outcome. A calm and enduring attitude can save further trouble to both the ill-affected and recalcitrant sufferer and to us.

Avoiding a broad daylight vampire is the wisest option. A resort to a spiritual healing technique which is most beneficial can help a harassed victim. In default, the services of a spiritual healer may be sought. Moreover, a careful observance of the techniques featuring in this book offers a preliminary background for self-confidence and immunity from external threats.

A ruthless ill-disposed person, whilst preying on a victim, does not care for explanation or reasoning and can hardly be scared off by a reproach or anger. Any such attempt makes him or her more aggressive. A quick perception as soon as the toxic warning is sent out is helpful. A face to face confrontation is of no avail. Third persons having no idea of the cause of the quarrel cannot tell who is a fool and who is not. Keeping off and running away wounds the vampire's pride and they start shouting: "Run, run…" provoking a confrontation. Overflowing with self-confidence they proudly proclaim their secret weapon: "I have not been to school, but I have brains."

Here we have an instance of our external reality. By some figment of imagination the rascal intervenes in our path, ready to spoil our good sense. At moments like these, we are on the verge of losing control. We can regain control applying the fourth law, "*The law of direction*", and especially the fifth law, "*We have the ability to put whatever thought we want into our mind.*"

3

Six Laws of Thought and of the Mind

First law: Thoughts are real powers.
Second law: The mind is a transmitter and receiver broadcasting and receiving thoughts.
Third law: The law of attraction. This signifies that the thoughts we think with emotion have a magnetism that attracts the contemplated circumstances to us.
Fourth law: The law of direction. This signifies we always think thoughts, but we have the ability to retain a certain thought or dismiss it.
Fifth law: We have the ability to put whatever thought we want into our mind.
Sixth law: Our internal world and our external world are connected.

"Thought is mind in motion; its effect will depend entirely on the mechanism to which it is attached."
Charles F. Haanel, *The Master Key System*

The Goods of our Personality

We can hardly ignore what goes on around us. We are connected to other people, as much as to the animal and the physical world. While connection to the latter remains fairly the same for all humans, our relationship to human beings is mostly governed by man-made rules. In the formation of these rules we play a tiny role, however insignificant, mostly in our private capacity and to a lesser extent we contribute to the formation of collective or public rules. This requirement happens to be so, because no one of us is a hermit or a Robinson Crusoe. Our interests and rights are at stake most of the time. Our will is the major drive in guarding our interests and rights and in developing the goods of our personality in a wider sense.

These goods include our personal freedom, our honour, our freedom of opinion and to the press, the protection of our home, private and family life, our health, dignity, the privacy of our correspondence, our intellectual property, bodily integrity, our right to participate in associations, right to make agreements, to exercise a profession or trade and others. It is important to bear in mind that society and the state offer means for the external protection of these goods, while the internal protection rests on our shoulders. This protection emanates from our internal initiative. Hence our internal world is of paramount significance when we come to consider the sixth law under this title, stating that "Our internal world and our external world are connected".

Living in a highly sophisticated society, such as our contemporary one, increases our burden and responsibility to remain alert and aware of modern demands. Admittedly, there is a distance between proclamations and practice, while mere chance or good fortune is not overflowing in a world of high complexity. Chance and fortune by definition work both ways. Sometimes they take away what we have accomplished with diligence and hard work.

Vigilance needs to extend to what is *acquis* and also to the ability to innovate by improving existing talents within the scope envisaged in this book. Our nervous system hosts our consciousness which operates to full capacity setting in motion our memory, perception, observation, imagination, judgement, visualisation, patience, ability to listen, to learn, to do mental and intellectual work, to endure incommodious conditions, to communicate, to negotiate and to synchronise with others. Fatigue, illness, frustration, negative earthly whirlpools and whirlwinds, may upset our mental equilibrium and disturb the efficient operation of our consciousness.

Lapse of consciousness under the influence of high fever, heavy drinking, or toxic substances may lead to temporary invalidity of a person's actions or omissions. Mental illness or disturbance of thinking-within-reason has its impact on the sufferer on a more permanent basis, whilst in between the two a prolonged addiction to drinking, narcotics, or profligacy have medium term effects on the goods of the personality.

Not being able to have a free will or to weigh the consequences of a binding expression of will lead to invalidity and thereby to inability to be a party to agreements. This affects both the receiving and transmitting end whilst the internal and external world of an individual eventually become disconnected. Damages, tutelage, custody, and wills are some of the institutions that take into account mental inabilities and provide respective regulatory arrangements.

4

The Conscious Mind

Our conscious mind is the seat of all wisdom and all knowledge. All knowledge begins when we become aware how many things we do not know.

The *conscious* mind deals with the impressions and objects of the outward life. It can discriminate, make choices and always conceives thoughts. However, it is a mechanism that conceives many useless thoughts. Undue anxiety, disquietude and fear are a few of these thoughts.

Fear of course has a certain role in our life. If we go into a cage with a tiger, then fear is indeed natural and necessary, as we may become food and energy for the tiger.

But sometimes we may lose control of this mechanism.

We can win back this control, as soon as we realise we have lost it or it is deceiving us, through useless thoughts. We can perceive undue anxiety, fear, anger or other negative feeling with the help of *self-observation.*

"All gain is the result of an accumulative consciousness.
All loss is the result of a scattering consciousness."
Charles F. Haanel, *The Master Key System*

Active Protection

Active protection of our bodily systems, including the support of our nervous system can be achieved through a number of disciplines available in the market.

These include a wide range of methods comprising physical exercise, diet, supplements reinforcing our health and biological coordination aids. They presuppose a certain expense, learning, programming and timing, but they have a unique advantage; they can be tailor-made to our individual needs, taking us from one grade to the next higher grade.

Adoption of such newly spreading disciplines is very slow owing to their innovative nature on the one hand and to the hesitant attitude and lack of open mindedness on behalf of most individuals on the other. Only a very small minority of persons have an enquiring mind and the daring to introduce new and more effective alternatives into their life. The expense and budgetary tightness is one reason that holds many back, but also the inconceivable difference between the old and the new means.

Sooner or later our conscious mind, as much as our bodily and mental strengths, will follow the orbit of decline. One does not need to be overwhelmingly preoccupied with this eventuality. However, a sustainable approach is preferable when compared to indolence and indifference to existing advantages, offering to us better synergies. Having in our quiver dynamic techniques enables us to eliminate mistaken impressions and assess our progress towards feasible targets. By moving from the theoretical stage to the practical we realise better outcomes and get the satisfaction intended from enhancing useful thoughts in our mind.

With self-observation and self-concentration we thus add value to our standards and quality of life. This may seem an invisible benefit, but it is not granted without some exertion on our behalf. For this, we do not need prompting or licence from others and do not have to give an explanation to somebody else, once we follow our creative plan, rather than waiting for an event to happen and then to react. In the course of time, a chain of more events follow, weakening our resistance and self-defence. Such a course is contrary to active protection which is within our reach.

Self-observation reveals to us the areas where we are about to fall behind or those areas where we run riot and therefore need a respective improvement or exercise of restraint. Achieving a midway between extremes requires self-control and discipline. These checks and balances are provided within the mind. The best known norms are dealt with in the Aristotelian essay on *Virtues and Vices*. Aristotle divides the soul in three parts reason, passions and appetites.

A midway between lower and higher extremes is also followed by modern medicine classifying a long list of indicators portraying the state of human health and the areas where the taking of measures is required. Self-observance is made possible by regular testing and adjustment. This very often necessitates a modicum of new discipline comprising the abandonment of old habits and their replacement with new ones.

5

Self-Observation
and Self-Concentration

The way to notice if you are losing control of any feeling is by using a technique called *self-observation*. You can achieve this technique, when you watch carefully and notice how you are thinking several times a day.

Look at yourself, as if you were a third person, observe how you are thinking and what this thinking is doing to you. If you do this several times a day, then very soon you will realise the conscious is continuously in motion. Continuously it cheats you and you always have useless thoughts in your mind.

The next technique we shall practice is *self-concentration*. Self-concentration is the most significant ability that you can bring into the working of your thought.

What is self-concentration? Self-concentration is a technique that improves your ability to focus all your attention to one point only, called the centre. When you unite together all your mental strength on one centre, it gains vivacity and liveliness that increases its intensity and effectiveness. The power of self-concentration can be compared to the power of a lens, where the rays of the sun are so strong that if you hold the lens steadily over a certain inflammable material, without moving it, the material burns.

"The subconscious relies upon the conscious mind 'the watchman at the gate', to guard it from mistaken impressions."
Charles F. Haanel, *The Master Key System*

The Network Puzzle

We are living in a turn of times in which most creative expectations have been down-sized. Hence, suggesting an alternative course will be looked at with a frown of disapproval. Creative power does exist, but is not channelled in the direction many benevolent planners envisage. Here, the chicken and egg question remains without an answer. Is it unwillingness that sets forth the inverse motion? Or is it inverse mindedness that did not match the trends and means?

In this book we are not concerned with collective orientations, but only with individual pursuits. In so far as individuals do not function singly, but only within a broader collective framework, their creative activities need to be integrated within a well knit together network When such a network collapses, the individual certainly remains deserted. No amount of creativity will suffice to recreate a defunct network. Networks are getting rarer in society and finding an equivalent one is a utopian fantasy. The incremental reward of creativity does not work hand in hand with the work of the hands or the labour of the body or even that of the mind.

Nevertheless, at the end of the day, the most creative persons, even though they may not get ahead as they were contemplating, may still be left with some groundwork affording them to survive the vicissitudes of fortune. A diligent and versatile person has a better chance to safeguard some modicum of stability zone and also to adapt to changing circumstances.

The most relevant question to ask here is: "What is my network?" This is designated within certain priorities and means. A network is liable to constant movement and change. We have active networks, which enable us to fulfil basic needs. We also have passive networks, which cater for secondary needs. Even passive networks can influence our creative force to some degree and give us an indication of social preferences and directions.

A good network is vital to all sectors of human activity. Essentially, the understanding of our particular network is a *sine qua non,* as it forms an integral part of our existence, whether we are involved in some kind of practical job or enjoy a conventional environment. All networks sooner or later present their ups and downs. The highest risk seems to be an innate part of entrepreneurial pursuits as commerce goes hand in hand with the risk of loss or damage due to transport, fire, theft, non-profitable disposal if goods, act of god and others.

Negative thoughts are of no avail in the carrying out of business. A more constructive attitude relies on taking practical measures aiming at the offsetting or mitigating of risks. Insurance schemes offer a wide range of coverage. Even before the initiation of a project, one can start with a feasibility study, research or seek the assistance of advisory services, thus preparing the ground before embarking on demanding project. Awareness of safeguards in the form of social, health and professional insurance is a good option.

6

The Conscious Mind:
A Very Lazy Person

At the beginning when you try self-concentration, you will find it difficult. The first two seconds will seem to be an hour. The reason for this is because you are not used to this technique. However, with practice, you will. It is like our body when we do not keep it fit by exercising. Likewise, our mind is untrained because we never exercise it. Our mind is very lazy. The only thing we do in life is to react.

In reality we never use our mind in depth; we only make calculations, react or analyse life without ever creating reality. With the techniques you are going to learn, you will be able to become creative and to work without reacting. You will be able to create your reality, exactly as you like it. It takes care and effort to unfold a nimble mind, quick and sharp to perceive what lies beyond the outer veneer of things. This care does not require strenuous and stressful stretching of the mind before reaching the stage of contemplation, which is the reward of a cultivated mind.

On the contrary, the effort works in the opposite direction, through *meditation*. Meditation is a most peculiar technique. All it requires is to get away from all stress and strain in the first place, but not only that.

The next stage of meditation is to devote a few minutes every day, as long as you can, during which you free your mind as much as possible from any intruding thoughts. By succeeding to keep thoughts away, for a stretch of time, you realise afterwards that your mind gets replenished with new energy and new ideas.

> **"Self-concentration is the highest accomplishment of every successful person."**
> **Charles F. Haanel, *The Master Key System***

Living in a Box

Within the context of this book apart from inward techniques that we exercise for our own pleasure and benefit, we can come in contact with other amateurs and sometimes with professionals who pursue similar or related scopes. We can compile our own library on this branch of interest that can help us expand our understanding and enable us to get nearer to our desired level of success. In due course, we may be able to notice our degree of progress in this domain. This progress does not exclude quantitative measurements but also takes into account the quality of life that we are able to enjoy.

We do not need to be alarmed when we see persons whose interests do not extend further than their dog and their nails. Others, who are interested in cooking and painting only or a great majority are passing their time watching television or playing games. A great many read books, but prefer novels, poems, or technical books relevant to their trade or business. Living in a box is a quite normal phenomenon. Not everybody needs to have a guitar and twang it after all. Even persons with multiple interests are limited by time and energy reserves to encompass all of them in their timetable.

Living in a box offers us certainty and security, like birds living in a cage. Birds in a cage are certain about their food and run much less risks from outside enemies as compared to free birds. Discovering new horizons through techniques that enter into our deepest recesses gives us a lead that sets us apart from our fellows. Life outside the box is lonely, setting us apart and far away from others. Even being together with others does not mean we necessarily connect with them as personal situations and interests are multifarious in our age and attention is limited.

Influences come from all sorts of directions channelled from a plethora of technological devices available to everybody. A degree of precedence is at stake at any time as well as a high demand for patience and sometimes endurance. Our feelings and will as well as our judgement and selective abilities are called to the front line more often.

On the other end of complacence we find people endowed with versatile and curious minds. Led by a restless desire, they do not refrain from pains and expense in endeavouring to explore new boundaries. They engage in expeditions through the land, sea and space. They are ready to climb Mount Everest or Mount Kilimanjaro or engage in underwater explorations.

With their dedication and self-denial they enriched human legacy and conferred incalculable benefits to their fellow human beings. What sets them apart is their own "I believe" and their own resourcefulness in the domain of the power of thought.

7

Contemplation

This technique can help you self-concentrate. It provides an excellent way to develop your mind. Whatever topic or thing you choose to think about, contemplation will give you the information about this topic or thing.

There are many different stages of knowledge and many different stages of perception. Knowing something on the surface may be cheating; one does not possess true knowledge. *Contemplation* is exactly the way to get beyond the surface and reach the real deep meaning and interpretation of each thing that you contemplate.

In a nutshell, to contemplate means to observe, look at, wonder and view something in depth. It also means to study, to examine, to foresee, and to anticipate. With systematic practice you will realise that strong and concentrated thoughts are dynamic and concentrated powers, while weak thoughts are weak and scattered powers.

Your mind is a station that transmits and receives these real powers. You must always know that you affect your environment with the thoughts that you think, and your environment affects you with the thoughts that it transmits to you.

"Knowledge does not apply itself; we as individuals must make the application."
Charles F. Haanel, *The Master Key System*

Innovation

Innovation is constantly pursued as an essential means of survival. By developing our thoughts we have an excellent instrument to keep ahead and discover new horizons. The impact of innovation is twofold. It's good for innovators enabling them to forge ahead, and may also be good for the recipients, by saving them time, expense or affording them a new advantage. A constant stream of innovation brings about an overflow to the rim and tiredness to constant change and adaptation on the part of recipients. Applying new knowledge is by no means as widely welcome as we may think.

Old masters continue to apply their long established methods, distrusting new products and methods. Very often new products and methods are mere alternatives, though sometimes they have evident advantages. Resistance to new knowledge is fantastically strong and indeed much stronger than we think. This leaves innovators highly disappointed while adherents get tired in their turn and sooner or later new knowledge is set aside, if not abandoned.

Distrust and fear of the unknown keep many away from evident improvements, even when their own health is concerned. In other fields, reactive attitude persists in the form of improvisation, which very soon is bound to wither away. New improvising reactions come to fill the space in an endless chain of paradoxes. Many people yearn for some desirable innovation that will bring wonders to the existing discontents which have mounted over the years. New fears and new anxieties present themselves in the process of time. Many individuals very often do not hide their disappointment and despair in the face of new hindrances blocking their way to their well-intended dreams and aspirations.

Still, no innovation can come about outside the conscious mind and contemplative process of an innovator. A flexible mind, well protected from negative thoughts is vital, while a good platform and a favourable network is indispensable.

It occurs sometimes in the form of a new idea, implement or method which comes to the mind spontaneously out of the blue. Or it may come as a corollary to the seeking of a solution to meet new obvious developments. Originality and more effectiveness are essential merits of innovation, but do not amount to invention as such. It can be initiated by one entrepreneur as an idea to bring about better efficiency, productivity or savings in his business, but very soon the whole industry can change its traditional outlook owing to the need to keep pace with modern requirements.

To the extent that modernisation occurs without detriment to any stake holder it can be welcome without any complaint or controversy. Sometimes it can be a source of jealousy or envy by others as in the case of the man said to pray that the goat of his neighbour dies because she yields more milk than his own. In other occasions, it may bring about ill will and manifestation of malice towards the innovator. This can be the case in which vested interests are affected. In this instance, it may be a cause of open reaction and a new contest or dispute among those involved. Thus response to innovation varies on the basis of benefits and interests at stake.

Very often a renovation project may be sought in a latent form retaining old features taking the form of re-antiquation or rehabilitation. This may be incidental to rising costs or come about as a matter of taste or convenience. A flexible attitude and a constant resort to contemplation as well as caution toward negative thoughts lend us a helping hand and enable us to stay ahead in this vanguard of progress.

8

Negative Thoughts

Every negative thought in your mind is there because you allow it to stay there.

Indeed, we have to ponder how many useless thoughts we keep in our mind that we should have dismissed long ago, and also how much insecurity, inferiority and pain we sometimes carry with us. One of the greatest powers we are endowed with is the ability to allow entry into our mind whatever thought and whatever kind of thought we like, without it yet being true or real. We know thoughts are truly actual powers. Nobody tells us how to think and what to think. Therefore, we can create our external reality, once our internal and our external worlds are connected.

Learn to understand the relationship that thoughts you are thinking have with situations happening to you. For this reason, you must be able to control and direct your thoughts, before you can control and direct the circumstances in your life.

"Substitute thoughts of fear, lack and limitation with those of courage, power, self-reliance and confidence."
Charles F. Haanel, *The Master Key System*

Mister Not Now

A strict self-discipline denotes a high degree of concentration to each task in hand. Attention to performance is a rewarding merit. However, a "Not Now" course, pursued to its utmost perfection, is a sign of over-caution. No room for "now" is on the other end of a scattered non-concentrated mind liable to loss resulting from a scattering consciousness. Going all the time in one way is on the whole speedier and safer. The urge for communication, one of the strongest in human beings is completely eradicated by Mister Not Now, setting him apart in a watertight compartment.

A prolonged "Not Now" state may take away some secondary pleasures which are of no importance to Mister Not Now himself, but may be a source of worry to those depending on his good services. As far as no detriment occurs, both sides are happy.

A consistent approach to communication and good time management skills become highly relevant to our performance. A strange and untrustworthy comrade in our team undermines not only our performance, but also our goodwill towards third persons. When we have discretion to opt out, it is much better to do so rather than compromise with undue stress, strain, sadness and other negative thoughts. When the opting out pros and cons are not in our favour, we take all possible measures to mitigate the damage done to us. Moulding our reality to a better footing requires patience, time and hope as well as a careful consideration of possible outlets from a commitment to an unwholesome project.

Unwinding is even harder, when someone is faced with an infatuation combined with fraudulent tactics. Social safeguards are very slow, while the cost is high and the ill effects are merciless and unwieldy. Our life is marked not only by thinking, but also by emotions and will. A loss of balance lurks at every turning and passage, with unforeseeable consequences. This is the worst type of personal affliction, because we admit an enemy into our own camp.

Procrastinating and putting off impending tasks can be a real menace to the interests of the other party engaged in an agreement. Postponing tasks to the last minute before a deadline becomes a source of unnecessary anxiety and fear of loss or irreparable damage. In a proverbial sense, procrastination is the thieve of time. We can do our best to improve our time management skills to enhance our productivity and sense of good order, though we may not have the means to extend this habit to others long used to follow a deviant path. Undoubtedly we cannot suggest to them that their mind seems to have become very lazy.

Good temper and stamina are essential tools. In practical terms, they are of great help when we are expected to deal with someone awkward. We often encounter persons possessing such remarkable abilities, while others pursue them through attending a public relation training. In this way, they acquire worthwhile knowledge understanding how to deal with varying characters and the qualities inherent in persons, adopting an appropriate attitude for each gender, as men are known to be able to tackle only one thing at a time, whilst women are said to have the ability to keep track, even when they seem to have a butterfly mind.

9
Know Thyself

What did Socrates mean when he said, "Know thyself"? Did he mean know how to write your name, address, your good points or bad points? Know what you like and what you dislike? No! What he meant was to understand in depth what and who you are, your abilities and your potential.

Practising this technique, you can understand you are the holder of a mechanism called 'mind'. This mechanism can bring whatever situation you like near you; it enables you to have the self-knowledge which allows you to know your strength and to use it.

In reality we need to measure the power of our mind. If we use always the same level of our mind, it is like driving a powerful car staying only in the first gear, ignoring how to change to the second or third gear. In the same way, we should not always use the same level of our mind. We must learn and understand how to make use of all our powers. We cannot see them, listen to them or touch them, but we can use them and introduce them in our daily life in the same way that we use a knife and fork.

"Dry dawn wisest soul"
Heraclitus

Self-Positioning

We derive our self-knowledge from a number of criteria. One such set is the duo objective versus subjective criteria. To the extent that the former are in good order, we have a formidable safeguard that protects our personal endowments as we have seen in page 18 of this book. A sound self-esteem coupled with commitment to success is bound to confer to us their due rewards. The creative forces and techniques propounded in this book pave the way towards this end.

The respective mind-control devices are also conducive to shield us from superficial and erroneous ideas and sentiments that irresponsible and sometimes arrogant persons address to us. As soon as we recognise the subjective nature of a remark or suggestion, we set in motion the appropriate mind-control technique that gives us instant protection with an irrevocable effect, neutralising and dismissing a target shot amiss.

In self-positioning we do not lose sight of conventional criteria, once we are content with our lot and appreciate our blessings.

In times when migration upheaval gains momentum, conventional criteria of self-definition become highly relevant. They comprise our name, gender, next of kin, domicile, nationality, health, honour, religion, educational qualification and membership in professional and prestigious organisations. We may take them for granted, but *faux pas* leading to deprivation or exclusion is highly undesirable and traumatic. Therefore utmost care to maintain and improve existing privileges is an essential condition for our wellbeing.

Beside these criteria, we are witnessing a rising technological evolution enabling us to collect more extensive and more accurate information about the function of our bodily organs and systems, including that of our brain. A sound mind resides in a sound body. As we get older, our bodily and mental faculties become weaker demanding more discipline on our behalf for their maintenance. No one else can replace our personal attention and care for this maintenance. By having access to the data involved, we gain better self-knowledge, we prop our ego in the good sense, boost our self-confidence and keep free from negative thoughts and feelings.

Portraying and regarding ourselves as a particular type of person is crucial in our teens. We have our initial choices and orientations at that particular phase of our life. Though we may not have any notion of the six laws of the thought and of the mind, they happen to be at play. Outcomes depend to a large extent on the type of society in which we find ourselves.

10

Cultivate Your Mind

Gain power exercising the techniques illustrated in this book. The mind is like a garden that can be cultivated or left uncultivated, and full of weeds. Your mind will be more productive with this care and treatment. Whatever thought enters is saved and you can nourish it and then it will grow. It will produce fruit.

If no good and useful thoughts enter your mind systematically, then many wild weeds or negative thoughts will grow, bringing many problems and difficulties into your life.

Because, whether with sound thoughts or wrong thoughts, your mind will produce according to whatever you give it. Therefore you must become a clever gardener. Start cultivating this mechanism as a clever gardener cultivates his garden. You can choose whether to turn it into a real masterpiece or neglect it and let it perish. Whichever choice you make, your life will reflect the state of your mind with great precision.

"We learn by doing; through practice the athlete comes powerful."
Charles F. Haanel, *The Master Key System*

The Survival of the Fittest

The phrase coined by Herbert Spencer, based on evolutionary theory by Charles Darwin, describes biological phenomena. These phenomena work in nature by virtue of a certain natural power called "Fitness". Developing our power of thought is a means by which we improve our mental fitness to cope with the exigencies of life.

Fitness implies also a quality of suitability for survival. When we are able to influence our fitness, we do not remain apathetic onlookers to random happenings but take the lead and have a say in the sequence of events. Thus, on the balance of advantages, the scales turn towards those who endeavour to cultivate their mind.

Fitness installations provide facilities to all fans of exercise ready to improve their bodily fitness. Most of them do so instinctively. Bodily exercise helps keep the mind at rest, as in the case of meditation, and promotes its replenishment with new ideas, provided these are sound and duly nurtured with proper cultivation of the mind aiming at an overall fitness. This fitness implies harmonious integration in the "immediate and local environment" to put it in the words of Darwin himself.

The fitness concept presents us a good analogy in the area of developing our thought. We need to strike a right balance between the stakes involved in each case. Say, we need enough money. We have a number of choices to achieve this objective. For example: work more or find a job with better remuneration. Or we can cut our spending or costs, etc. Then we have to consider the impact of work on our health, or maybe the impact of work on our desire to find a better job, or on our family needs and commitments.

Once we choose to live a simple life and have certainty, we cannot expand too far upwards because then uncertainty creeps in, nor too far to the right, because complexity increases. Thus, as our curve moves upwards and rightwards our development or survival along the upward curve becomes more precarious. The pros and cons of our environment have a bearing on us and on our decisions and choices. A sound organised complexity provides a favourable background, while a random complexity is less trustworthy.

11

Achieve Your Targets

If you are not happy with what is happening in your life, if you have targets you would like to achieve, then you must start looking inside this mechanism and think what thoughts you have planted. Because if you do not like the harvest, then you need to think about the kind of seeds you planted that led you to where you are today.

If you like to produce corn, sow corn seeds. It is very natural. Let us now have a look at your life.

You need, say, enough money, but you continually worry that there is not enough for your needs. You need abundance, but you think of scarcity.

You desire to be cured from an illness, but you continually think you are getting sick. You desire health but you think of illness.

You desire to find a good job, but you continually think it is difficult to find such a job.

By cultivating your mind, you can think independently and beyond what your immediate situation and circumstances suggest, and you can set and pursue the target that will be your guiding star.

"A life without an aim is dull and uncertain."
Seneca, *Ad Lucil. Epist. 95*

What is a Skill?

A skill is the ability to do something expertly and well, thus becoming an excellent artist. We have simple skills which almost everybody can do, e.g. walking, running, cycling, rowing and other similar repetitive movements. Skills composed of multiple movements require a longer time and regular training to become familiar to the expert artist or performer. This ideo-kinetic nature of skills makes possible their automatic performance at the order of the mind and will.

Many performers limit themselves to one or to as few skills as possible. As a rule adherence to one skill or to as few as possible leads to improved performance while expansion to a wider range lowers the standard of performance. This does not exclude many multi-skill persons engaging in a wider range of skills on their own initiative. In recent times, circumstances change very frequently, making it inevitable for many skilled persons to have to make a move to another skill. As a consequence, a more flexible attitude is necessitated.

Weighing the scales between better performance and an adaptable profile is a frequent dilemma. The Six Laws of the Thought and of the Mind emerge in such critical moments of quandary. A close familiarity favours the performer faced with perplexity or even bewilderment to find the answer.

Skill performers are governed by competitive norms classifying them into winners and losers. This norm prevails when a competition is closed where one person wins at the expense of others (zero-sum competition). In an open competition, all persons can increase their gains and get more cake, without any expense to each other.

They are also governed by migratory rules classifying them into five tiers for purposes of a work permit in another country:

Tier 1 comprises highly skilled workers, entrepreneurs, investors.

Tier 2 is divided into four categories. 1.) General, for a job offer. 2.) Intra-company transfers for employees of multinational companies. 3.) Sports performers for significant contribution to upgrade their sport to a higher level. 4.) Ministers of religion for the purpose of filling a vacancy.

Tier 3 is for the securing of a visa to unskilled temporary migrants.

<u>Tier 4</u> is for students.

<u>Tier 5</u> is for temporary workers, granted for purposes of a holiday visa.

Competitors in the skills arena can succeed by gaining some competitive advantage. Those who stay behind need to confront an unpleasant outcome and also have the courage to direct their energy towards another option by finding another cake or cheese when hit by overwhelming adversity. Many proceed through the five tiers instinctively or as a matter of good luck, while others do so not losing sight of their blessings.

12
Exercises

Therefore, if you like corn, sow corn because whatever thought enters your mind will produce a related harvest. The power of the mind is to think your thoughts independently and over and above what the existing situation and circumstances suggest. If you wish to succeed in your life, then you must begin feeling happy. If you expect to feel happy only after you succeed, it may never happen. If you wish for personal power, health and success, then you should start cultivating your mind now.

Exercise 1: Every night, take a clean sheet of paper, write down the six laws and for five minutes think deeply, contemplating the six laws, their meaning and what they want to say.

Exercise 2: Take one law every night and think deeply about this law for five minutes.

Exercise 3: Every night contemplate the following sentence for five minutes: "I am the holder of an astonishing power mechanism which can convert my life, from the moment that I learn how to use it."

Exercise 4: Write down and consider this sentence: "My life and my thoughts are bundled together. My personal vibration, or pulse and energy from my thoughts, define the situations and circumstances that are happening to me."

"So much good method and connection may improve the common and the plainest things."
Horace, *Ars Poetica*, 242

Life is Motion

In due course, assimilating the mind-and-thought-laws becomes part of our super-ego. We apply this knowledge and judgement to the occurrences taking place in our everyday life in the course of our relationships with others. Apart from the theoretical background, we can become aware of our creative plans and of the response in their handling, both by us and by those involved in each process. Carrying out any programme depends on the degree of flexibility we encounter. One of our tasks is to check our creative course itself, and the relevant productivity and output.

We can make use of well-known indicators in each case, such as the strengths, weakness and also opportunities and threats; known as SWOT analysis and often used by organisations in the implementation of their projects. The human environment around us has its own SWOT indicators, enabling us to feel the pulse and evaluate our possible progress. We can do this diagnostic exercise at regular intervals and take corrective measures where necessary. Keeping our cool and working harmoniously is a great strength which we should be able to employ.

Negative feelings stem primarily from an inflexible environment having the tendency to transmit to us aggressive energy, because of unfolding difficulties before us. We instantly feel our blood pounding in our head, our breathing coming to a halt, our expression becoming miserable, our heart beats at a faster pace and our feet and knees freeze. Prolonged ordeals fill us with evident exasperation, anxiety, and awe. It's like a banana bunch hanging on the ceiling in a monkey enclosure. Whenever a monkey climbs the ladder to get hold of a banana a mechanism is set in motion, showering all the monkeys in freezing cold water. Confronting this dilemma, the monkeys abstain from their instinctive and strong desire to satiate their hanger. When one monkey is released from the enclosure and replaced by another, the new monkey spontaneously is about to climb the ladder, but the other monkeys do not let him do so. Their aversion to cold keeps them from their desire to enjoy a banana relish.

13

Attitude

As a rule, the creative power of thought is accessible to you, as it is to all human beings, and you make use of it every day of your life. When you are successful, you have your internal and external world in harmony; but sometimes you may realise that you are facing problems and difficulties. Nevertheless, unfavourable situations and circumstances should not dominate your internal world, because you have full control of what is happening in your mind. You have the strength and the ability to put in your mind whatever thoughts you want. And thoughts, you should always remember, are real powers.

Nothing comes about without effort, and this effort is certainly required from you. Keeping in check your mental attitude is what makes the difference. All successful people have this capacity, even sometimes without being aware of it. What they know is that it is effective, and that it can produce results. You can send out your message and collect what you need to fulfil your desire. Nothing can materialise without passing first in the form of a thought from your mind, which provides vision and imagination. You can also reverse this process by cutting out negative thoughts that you do not need; thoughts you can notice by employing self-observation.

As your thinking process obeys the rule, "As above, so below", each desire is mirrored in the outcome of each thought. That's why it is essential to pay attention to your mental attitude in order to succeed in your targets and be able to enhance your personality, your health, your happiness or your image.

> **"In order to express abundance, you must think abundance."**
> **Charles F. Haanel, *The Master Key System***

Desire and Aversion

So, as it has been said, life is motion between desire and aversion or even motion between pleasure and pain. Striking a balance within the elements of nature is one of the foremost existential games to which humans comply through common sense, avoiding harmful extremes. They avoid undesirable symptoms from exposure to extremities: for example, dehydration from drought, sunstroke from scorching sunshine, sunburn from ultra-red sun rays and discomfort from humidity, respiratory problems from dust, smoke, soot or poisonous fumes. They take shelter and do not expose themselves to cold, being a serious threat to good health.

Life, being a limited condition, exists between certain bounds that have to be observed. The degree of precaution varies from one person to another, but nobody is invulnerable or outside bounds. Resistance to health hazards coming from minuscule germs, designated as microbes, belong to categories known as viruses, bacteria, fungi, protozoa and other parasites that assail the organs and systems of the human body, is carried out by the immune system. As long as this system operates successfully, our health is protected.

Common sense itself, though operated individually, relies on a value system shared by society at large which in its turn is based on modal logic. This part of the mind comprises three specific values: command, permission and prohibition. And then modal logic itself has to take into account simple logic comprising two values only: true and false. Thus knowledge, ignorance and error intervene in guiding and forming intentions which in their turn lead to actions. Lack of consciousness, mental illness and drunkenness are three of the main causes that disconnect a person from the external world.

Someone being in such a state is deemed as irrational, but in real terms such person is classified as irresponsible, unable to be charged with responsibility and hence is taken into some kind of custody.

14

Alertness and Diligence

You should remember that for the mind there is no difference between a positive and a negative thought. The mind works with whatever material you give it, or if you neglect it, it will work only with the energy it receives from the situations and circumstances around you. And, if you observe, the society in which we live today is full of negative energy. If you do not attract positive thoughts and positive energy to your mind, you will continually absorb the negative energy found around you, and you will not be able to achieve the things that you want.

Therefore, be alert to the things that you like. They are going to happen only if you start cultivating your mind and turn away the negative thoughts. You can use four techniques to expel the negative thoughts from your mind:

First: Uprooting   Second: Observation

Third: Exaggeration.   Fourth: Neutralisation

"I think, therefore I am."
—Descartes

Our Stability Zone

Stability is a neutral term, as much as equality. Nobody likes equality in misery. Both notions are valuable under a fairly organised complexity, but detestable when random complexity prevails for causes lying outside the ambit of a person's perception. Under such vicissitude of fortune many an individual has to overcome negative outcomes with their own ingenuity as best they can.

When a robber takes the treasure, he throws away the treasure box. The dutiful mother collects the empty box. She recycles her stability zone by creating a new treasure to afford her children a commodious living in the future.

The most important pillar for stability for individual persons happens to be the family. Then there comes a list of qualities, abilities and conditions, and of immaterial goods used for the identification of the person, but also relating to the nature of a human being as a superior creature. These constitute a net of ideal values, which endow the person and complete the person's physical, social, and particularly, moral status.

Such qualities or values comprise the name, image, honour, dignity, purity, bodily integrity, goodwill, and others. Their protection is achieved within an open competition, where, as we have seen in Chapter 11, all persons can increase their gains and get more cake, without any detriment to others.

Good conduct attracts mutual respect and generates positive energy. Positive energy is a vital force sustaining our wellbeing in a positive way. In Chapter 13 we have already seen two hazards to health, one from natural extremities and another from an array of microcosm creatures. In this chapter, we have a subtle kind of negative energy tending to undermine our positive outlook coming from the bully. In a wider selection, such an occurrence is statistically inevitable.

A bully may delay an urgent communication for immediate action, thrive on finding an imaginary fault or postpone a pending matter for no evident reason. One good protection is to keep records of important matters. Another is to, "Take care of one's own mother"; that is avoid doing anything that may cause one's mother to cry. As the saying goes, "Instead of my mother, let your mother cry" and a third one is, "Tie the donkey where they tell you and let him die".

15

Uprooting

Uprooting is a simple technique of vigilance as to what type of thought you are thinking. With this technique, as soon as you notice that you are thinking a negative thought of doubt, fear, distrust or other thought of discouragement, you must instantly stop and replace it with a positive thought of hope, courage, trust and encouragement.

Do not react to the negative thought by analysing, weighing or by trying to think if it is right or wrong.

Instead, as soon as you notice what is happening in your mind at a given moment, realising that you are thinking a negative thought, you instantly stop it and replace it with a positive thought. If you realise you are thinking of sickness, cast sickness away and think of health. Affirm to yourself that you are fit, perfect, strong, powerful, loving, harmonious and happy.

"The only way to keep from going backward is to keep going forward."
Charles F. Haanel, *The Master Key System*

A Successful Mindset

A mindset reflects a number of capabilities of the mind. Thus we have an adjective "mental" that describes a number of abilities and conditions classifying a person accordingly. Then we have a noun such as "mentality" measuring degree of intellectual power. For example average, high or low, or a characteristic attitude of mind such as "a bulling mentality" as we have seen in Chapter 14. We also have a long list of expressions relevant to memory. Mind also refers to wishing, opinion, intention, purpose, decision making, doubtfulness, determination. We have also presence or absence of mind, right mind or wrong mind.

Moreover, we have a verb "to mind" which refers to paying attention, carefulness, noting, affirmation, negation, objection and worry or absence of worry. We have also another adjective "minded" denoting disposition, inclination or character such as strong minded, high minded or evil minded and additionally consciousness of the importance or value of something. Furthermore a "minder" is a person entrusted a specific duty.

A "mindful person" is one giving thought and attention to some duty, while the opposite is "mindless" person or action.

All these expressions are significant when we are revising our exercises or when we use or practise one of the four techniques related in Chapter 14 up to 19. Bound together they offer an instant mind control aid on a regular basis. This aid is valuable when we consider suggestions and opinions addressed to us by others. What we need is the courage and dexterity to navigate the right course without falling into a trap or tripping up.

After all, what we do is to employ our mental resource to an upgraded level. Our measure of success is the last criterion to be considered in due course; besides, we should not lose sight of the fact that we are simply complying with the demands and progress of the age we are living in. One cheering note about this progress is that we have the means to observe the function and the energy level of our bodily organs including those of the brain which hosts our mind.

16
Observation

Become the observer of negative thoughts. As soon as you notice a negative thought coming into your mind, examine it and qualify it. What you must know is that negative thoughts acquire strength only if you react to them, or keep them. If you do not react to them, or keep them, they have no strength and they cannot harm you.

Therefore, when you notice that a thought is negative, make note of it but say simply that this thought is negative, and pay no more attention to it.

When you notice you are thinking negatively, say to yourself, "This is not going to happen," or "It cannot happen" or "I should not think of it." Then you should know that it is not going to affect you.

Moreover, endeavour to get positive thoughts and positive energy in your mind. Positive thoughts and positive energy shield you from absorbing or internalising negative energy that is found around you.

"Experiences come to us through the law of attraction brought into operation by our predominant mental attitude.
Charles F. Haanel, *The Master Key System*

Mind in Motion

Thought, being mind in motion, performs an unbelievable number of tasks. It observes attentively, pays attention, examines, takes into account, weighs probabilities, counts, measures, calculates, computes, judges, reaches conclusions, studies, keeps in mind, considers, recalls, reflects, evaluates, classifies, imagines, suggests, forms opinions, recognises, analyses, solves problems, plans, makes providence, compares, negotiates, remembers, conceives ideas, perceives, estimates and many others. Such performance may be positive or negative and is valid as far it is true, but invalid when it happens to be false or erroneous.

Scepticism is an attitude of mind of persons doubting the truth of a statement, claim, theory, etc. Though sceptical means originally thoughtful or deep in thought, it has come to mean such an attitude, or someone inclined not to believe. Second thoughts can sometimes be better, depending on the outcome. Who would like to be wrong? The art of reaching right conclusions is a worthwhile pursuit by a prudent person. Deep thinking on difficult problems spoils grey matter, while too much thinking ails the boss. In contrast, a thoughtless conduct leaves the mind intact, in the case of a boss who does not use his temples, "*Il ne s'use pas se méninges,*" or does not strike a tune.

Science is recognised to be the knowledge of consequences. As such it is obtained by observation and testing of facts arranged in an orderly manner. Most accomplished scientists reach a high level of performance relying on a cultivated and developed mind. Inspiration is a merit leading to creative activity through good thoughts or ideas that come to the mind. Talented persons possess this blessing, besides their natural inclination towards a particular discipline in music, acting, painting, sports, dancing and other arts requiring focus and unceasing practising. Forethought and planning are manifest in building jobs, maintenance, repairs, paintings, as well as in decorative jobs, paving with flagstones, fountain building and arrangement works.

Know-how, expertise and specialisation are marks of a cultivated mind able to cope with specific demands in a given time and place denoting practical ability adapted for a particular purpose. The expert understands the causal laws through study and learning. The difference between a layman and an expert is an initiation in the causes and effects in a series of happenings and facts; because *each preceding event can be discerned from the most recent.* *[1]

---

[1] *Quote from Demosthenes

17

Exaggeration

With this technique, as soon as you notice you are thinking negatively, you begin to exaggerate the thought and this takes away its strength.

For example, let us suppose you are trying a new cake recipe. As your mind in most cases cheats you by introducing doubts, you begin to fear that probably the cake will not be successful. As a result you may be worried, especially if you are expecting visitors. That is, generally negative thoughts of failure begin to penetrate your mind, without any justified reason.

At this point, you can outwit negative thoughts by exaggerating. You start thinking that the cake will probably be a disaster, all of it will spill onto the floor or grease will flow onto the carpet. The neighbours will learn about it, and many other unsubstantiated exaggerations. Then your mind will begin to say no, no! These things are not possible! You say, "I will manage!" You assure yourself you will manage.

You see your mind often tries to make you believe the opposite of what you wish. It knows how to cheat you. Nevertheless, you can restore your self-confidence with the help of exaggeration.

"If you wish to eliminate fear, concentrate on courage."
Charles F. Haanel, *The Master Key System*

Inanity

Inanity, being lack of sense, occurs as an error in judgement, lack of discernment or inconsiderateness or thoughtlessness. It's the exact opposite of good judgement. When a series of events reaches a critical mass point, we perceive such a negative point as escalating in crisis. Nonetheless, by way of pun a humorously disposed comment infers lack of. Inanity is sometimes referred to as light-mindedness, a mental condition revealing emptiness of mind. This may be a harsh critique. As a rule, good manners do not allow an open, face to face remark, because having in mind the purported standard of a person we refrain from speaking our mind. We simply keep such remark to our conscious level, or reveal it in private, once we have grounds to prove our viewpoint.

However, having a developed standard of understanding we are able to perceive such instances when they come to our attention, when a dispute or controversy arises. The question at stake is how far this controversy affects our interests and rights and how far we choose to be indignant. A light-minded conduct may not be as bad as paranoia which is worse showing some kind of deviation from sanity. Light-mindedness may be due to some complex syndrome of superiority. Such instances occur in real life; therefore, we should not be surprised with this phenomenon.

As far as good judgement is a blessing, inanity is a defect to be avoided. When it comes to jesting, it may be harmless; after all life might be dull without some jesting in a good humoured background. When thoughtlessness runs out of proportion, it becomes a matter for concern, not only when personal relationships are at stake, but also when as collective phenomenon it affects the lives and wellbeing of a wider section of society. Especially when furious emotions are predominating or when someone strong-willed takes the lead; and even when calculated interests disregard the common good.

Under a frantic condition or a violent wrath thoughtlessness prevails with scaring escorts, anxiety, fear, resentment, rancour, despair and unhappiness. When a crisis is already a *fait accompli* resorting to the technique, we deem most suitable comes to us by way of logical necessity. Because at such a moment, we encounter an "alluring ritual" and may intuitively look to restore a magic philtre or philtre of love that has turned into a deadly poison. Though we can be much better off when we cultivate our mind and have the poise to combat negative thoughts by practising consistently.

18
Neutralisation

This technique is about neutralising a negative thought with an opposite positive thought. That is, as soon as you think that your cake will fail, you should immediately say that you are able to bake good cakes and you are going to succeed. In this way, you neutralise the negative thought by bringing in an argument with an opposite positive thought.

What is significant is that you can think one thought at a time. We may believe that we think many thoughts simultaneously, but what really happens is that one thought follows the other. Therefore, if you assure yourself that you can do a job you chose to do in your stride, you replace the negative thought with an opposite positive thought, and then the negative thought instantly loses its power.

Neutralisation is an effective and reliable technique. It helps you cultivate your mind and combat negative thoughts instantaneously.

"Thought is a mode of motion and is carried by the law of vibration the same as light or electricity."
Charles F. Haanel, *The Master Key System*

Savoir Faire

Savoir Faire refers to social tact, as to how to behave in society. We scarcely notice this aspect of interface with others. As know-how it happens to be so vast and may be impossible to master in our lifetime. Time and energy are not boundless. We can do our best through good organising and preserving our energy to best possible yield. We pick up the basics at an early age and add increments in accordance with the time and social environment we happen to have around us.

Some persons are more proficient, others need to work harder to increase their output and others may not be so favoured by the deities of luck.

In this book, we have the best guidelines to assist us in the unceasing race of *savoir faire.* We remember the six laws guiding our movements like expert chest players and remember our motto, "Create – Don't React." *Savoir Faire* begins with good manners and begins in the home. We remember to be thankful to the deities, our bringing up, and our intuitive achievements. Good manners include the forty commandments of good conversation.*[2] Walking matters in *savoir faire.* We wear comfortable shoes appropriate for each occasion. Diet is a matter of concern to many. How we eat? How we dress?

We do not forget etiquette in matters of *savoir faire.* Returning a greeting, the way we dress, a civil conduct towards others and other such matters fall within etiquette. Etiquette rules are not binding and are not coercive. Compliance is left to the individual; but noncompliance leads to general contempt. Contempt plays a very important role in social life as far as the keeping of etiquette is concerned.

Ethics are even more important than etiquette. Most corporations have ethical standards obligatory for their members based to a large degree on modal logic which we have seen in Chapter 13. Noncompliance may lead to expulsion or other disciplinary punishment. A similar rhythm prescribed by others, but having some degree of autonomy, applies to religious ethics. Thus we have Christian Ethics, Moslem Ethics, Hindu Ethics and others forming a system of rules that claim compliance by the faithful. Social ethics govern social

---

[2] *Savoir Vivre – *Good Manners for a Better Life* by
Ελένη Χαλκούση

behaviour as an aggregate of moral commandments based on concepts formed by society.

They constitute positive morality on what is moral and what is immoral. In social ethics, we have a more rigorous heteronomy that claims compliance. Moral judgement does not necessarily depend on the motive of will. It comprises elementary rules of social life independent from religious beliefs, not identical to rules prescribed by but much closer to the law.

19

Practise Consistently

We have just looked into four techniques:

UPROOTING,   OBSERVATION,

EXAGGERATION   NEUTRALIZATION

These techniques are completely different and independent from one another. It is up to you to choose the most appropriate as your situation requires.

Therefore, see which one is suitable in each particular situation. Choose the one you find appropriate and start using it to cultivate your mind. Dismiss every negative thought that you encounter.

Because, if you do not consciously work with this mechanism, the greater the likelihood that your "garden" will be full of weeds.

In short, practise these techniques, to avoid a life with problems and difficulties.

"Mind shapes and controls matter. Every form which matter takes is but the expression of some pre-existing thought."
Charles F. Haanel, *The Master Key System*

Ethics

Ethics comprises ethical rules emanating from the human conscience possessed by individual persons. Ethics constitute an autonomous rhythm. Under the principle of autonomy we obey our own conscience and not any rule dictated by another person. The modally moral, as to what we do or not do, comes from our own conscience. Our conscience is the law giver and judge of our actions.

The moral value of our action does not depend on what we are doing, but from which conscience we are doing this action. Our action is moral when it emanates from our free will obeying the moral law and not motives alien to the moral law. Ethics relying on the principle of autonomy is founded on the idea of the good as a value on its own merit. Hence an action is ethical or moral only when it is directed towards what is good.

Ethics concern our internal behaviour. Our behaviour is revealed by our actions determined by our will and brings about a change in the external world, physical or conventional. Action differs from instinct as determined by our will. An action is external when we have a change in the external world or is internal when we have a change in our internal world. An omission emanating from our will is an internal action, as showing our will not to engage in an action, for example, when we do not help someone who is in danger. In this kind of an omission, not directed towards what is good, law steps in. We see here an instance where our internal and external worlds are connected as envisaged by the sixth law, in Chapter 3.

Charity falls within the realm of ethics taking into account our will to help our neighbour, evaluating why we give our help. When our conscience follows the moral norm to help our neighbour, then our action is moral, but when our action is due to other motives our action is not deemed to be moral. However, as regards moral evaluation, we start from the internal world to reach the external manifestation of an action, for the purpose of evaluating the internal part of our behaviour.

Ethics aim at the realisation of the idea of what is good and lie within our freedom of thought. Ethics is also closely related to the idea of the law as the law assumes that participants rely on ethics: to live honestly, not to inflict harm on others and to give to every man what belongs to him, the latter precept coinciding with the idea of justice.

20

Feel the Difference

Your thoughts, your pulse and your vibrations matter. You can feel the difference between two opposite kinds of thinking. Look at these two series of thoughts:

First	Second
SELF-CONFIDENCE	LOSS
WELLNESS	FAILURE
SUCCESS	BAD LUCK
HAPPINESS	ANXIETY

I want you to follow these two different kinds of thinking. Let us look at the first series first. When you have them in your mind, what you are going to notice is that vibrations have their starting point. You feel these vibrations originating from your chest or head. On the contrary, when you have the second series of thoughts in your mind, you feel the vibrations originating from another point further down near the stomach. This realisation is important. How can this be? After all, what you are doing is only thinking some thoughts; unless, of course, thoughts are real powers. Let us follow two possible powerful techniques: SEEDING and VISUALIZATION. You can have them at your disposal to use in your everyday life. They bring about whatever you wish to happen.

"Fear is a powerful form of thought. It paralyses the nerve centres thus affecting the circulation of the blood."
Charles F. Haanel, *The Master Key System*

The Law of Vibration

The notion of good pervades the whole study of ethics. Indeed, as Aristotle observes, *"Every art and every method and likewise every action and choice are deemed to aim at some good. Hence, it has been well said that the good is that at which all things aim."* Thus, when we develop our power of thought we add incremental strength to the already existing force of our mind to make it even more dynamic. Why do we do this? One reason is because we realise that negative vibrations pulsating around us tend to diminish our strengths and our freedom and another reason is because they tend to restrict our forward movement.

We need to combat negative thoughts because they constitute an enemy within and we also need to reinforce our strengths so as to be able to forge ahead. We have already seen some sources of negative or static thoughts, the latter being of a stunting nature restricting our success. In the chapters that follow, we assume a more active role in this undertaking, which requires a more positive attitude. Once we have weathered negative threats, we prepare the ground for such changes in the external world that we require for our wellbeing. However, the law of vibration works towards both directions. We have already seen this little nasty parasite nesting in our liver or an assembly of bacteria finding accommodation in our mouth and throat cavity.

Once we locate them, we start ripping them out with any means we have at our disposal, following the law of vibration. We deprive them of their favourite toxins that give them food to thrive on and treat them with their corresponding frequency. Tiny beasts called viruses can cause fever, diarrhoea, headache and pain. When negative frequency comes from a person, we follow a very ancient motto: "Do not speak to bad people". For, this kind of negative frequency is not something new under the sun.

Those affected realised some kind of current is disturbing their train of thought or some other organ in their body causing them an ill feeling. Because, when we get upset, toxins have a propensity to multiply and parasites find food and thrive also. One good reason we should pay attention and not get in trouble is not to give rise to a vicious circle. Certainly, all is easy to tackle when we have no commitment towards a bad guy. We do not look around for trouble. But sometimes it may be harder when a person happens to be a necessary evil, somewhere in the hierarchy, or even doing a menial job. We cannot move the guy and we cannot move ourselves. There we have a bit of dilemma.

21

Seeding

"Seeding" is very powerful. When you master it, you will be able to achieve whichever situations and circumstances you wish in your life. Though powerful, seeding is simultaneously very simple.

Seeding is a technique that means sowing seeds in your mind. It works in the same way that we sow a piece of land with seeds, from which we get full grown plants. In figurative speech, for example, we often say, "Don't sow the seeds of hatred!" or "Sow the seeds of love!"

There is a distinct way we sow our thoughts. Just for a short while, pretend you are a great football player and you are poised to participate in a very important game. You are going to play with some of the best football players in the world and your team is going to win.

What I want you to do, most of all, is to experience this sensation; feel that your team is going to win this game. You are going to win, you know it; you feel this great excitement. Communicate with this feeling and notice how you feel when you are a winner.

"Of fire is the force these seeds have in them, divine is the source of their being."
Virgil, Æneas, VI 730

Electromagnetic Influences

The earth itself is also a palpitating entity carrying an earthly magnetic field, pipes of energy, condensers, transformers and accumulators. Old seasonal rituals were planned and maintained, having a useful function, to bring about the increase of the underground magnetism and from this magnetism the growth of the plants and the increase in the vitality of human beings. They did this with the pulsating vibrations of music and hymns for the sake of their life and their progress. Earth also emits negative "geo-radiation" which bursts from nuclear ruptures coming from the centre of the earth. Places from which such negative energy is emitted are known as sickly locations and can be found with the feng sui method.

The flow of cosmic energy to the human body for beneficial purposes could be achieved in the old days through cyclical dancing and the building of temples for mental and bodily wellness. In the human body, and as we have seen in Chapter 3, the brain is an electromagnetic receiver and transmitter which receives and emits electromagnetic waves, feels and sends with actions and thoughts respectively. The vital cosmic energy could run freely through a standing position with the feet on earth and the head turned upwards towards the sky. For the right internal allocation of the vital cosmic energy people in the know exercised their body in the gymnasium, and for the external allocation they built temples in the right places as means of acupuncture on the land. Such places corresponded to the nervous centres of the human body, the "chakras" known by the Hindus.

They were known for their therapeutic and fertile qualities. The megaliths operated as spools for the concentration and maintenance of the benefits of cosmic radiation. In due course, their efficiency in the healing of bodily and psychological diseases attracted visitors and in this way the institution of pilgrimage started to develop.

The land is run through by an electromagnetic field, which vibrates by a current of low tension. Conception itself takes place through the release of a biological electrical wave. All species of animal and plant systems are also run through by constant electromagnetic currents inside them.

Thus, desiring to achieve our ends, we cannot ignore the earthly and heavenly forces at work, while at the same time we should be ready to keep away from the negative energy and exploit the positive energy available by understanding nature around us.

22

Communicate with This Feeling

Communicate with this feeling; you *are* going to win this game! Now, I want you to make a little change. For a moment reverse your attitude and communicate with the opposite feeling: Say, "My team is going to lose this game," and, "We are not going to win." Try to capture how you feel, when you believe your team is going to lose this game.

Next, repeat your winning thoughts again, and feel that your team is going to win. Next, feel you have actually won the game. The game is over; your team is a winner. Feel this victory! Simulate this feeling. Pay attention to this detail; notice how all tension is gone and you feel at ease. A second requirement of this technique is that you need to bring to your mind these seeding thoughts very often and every day.

It is the power of repetition that makes this technique very dynamic. If every day you think how to achieve something or how to get something, it may succeed or it may not; because this is merely positive thinking. Seeding goes beyond positive thinking, asserting in your mind the feeling you have already acquired what you have sown. You need to grasp this point very well.

"All possession is the result of the accumulative attitude of mind."
Charles F. Haanel, *The Master Key System*

Random Complexity

Acts of God, otherwise known as natural disasters, indicate very often the negative effects of the globe in which we are hosted. Thus, we have tsunami, hurricanes, floods, earthquakes, tempests, blizzards, volcano eruptions and other similar phenomena which bring sudden devastation to many people from time to time. Despite the progress in forecasting devices and methods that we have at our disposal, we are still confronted with such happenings. Also many unchecked human activities bring about toxic rain, pollution, nuclear contamination, clouds of dust particles, and land desertification.

We have nine categories of dangerous goods moving along the roads and ports. These categories include toxic, corrosive, flammable, nuclear, explosive, chemicals and other goods, which need expert handling at all times, because they constitute a threat to human beings and the environment.

Dangerous goods have always been in the hands of warriors, from time immemorial, ranging from the humble sling and primitive bow to the most sophisticated weapons and missiles in our times. War is the apex point of aggression and the cause of bloodshed, death, mutilation and all sorts of destruction and loss; it has been depicted by great historians and gave food for inspiration to many literary masters of all ages. It is one of the most complex engagements. Apart from military equipment it employs, threat, fear, blackmail, violence and other similar macabre notions including atrocity and horror. Undoubtedly, if good luck matters once in times of peace, in times of war it matters a million times. In general, randomness and adventurism are not part of winning attitude and do not fall within the context of aiming at some good.

Nonetheless, strategy, being the art of an army general, is a very popular term and has been transferred very successfully to all walks of human achievement. Human choices aiming at some good are part of positive attitude. With careful planning a good project comes to fruition. Good order and logical sequence are essential components of seeding in emulating the dynamism and divine energy of the seed. The stages of growth and ripeness are bound to follow. Apart from intention, success is also favoured by absence of negligence. These two attitudes are the practical preconditions of liability in offences and accidents.

Such incidents are a matter of concern within the realm of organised complexity leading to certainty as opposed to random complexity which is the mother of uncertainty, and hence of anxiety and fear.

23

Visualisation

Visualisation is equally as dynamic as seeding. With visualisation you bring or recall the view of a person or thing and you see it with your mind. You use your mind's eye, to see something that has not yet happened.

By projecting in your mind what you want to see happening in external reality, you create a plan for the universe to follow. Whatever you see in your mind, you must try to see it clearly.

Let us say, you need to make a presentation or speech before an audience. Visualise yourself doing all these activities and see the people applauding and congratulating you. Feel that joy and satisfaction. See this in your mind as if this has already happened to you. Every time that you have this vision, the image of it happening becomes clearer. The clearer the image becomes in your mind, the greater and the more vigorous your power becomes.

"The material for the construction of your mental image is secured by your brain cells."
Charles F. Haanel, *The Master Key System*

The Better Life

The idea of good life had been the subject of debate among philosophers and philosophical schools time and again. The models of good life abound around us, while whatever the station at which individual persons or societies, small or extended, are found, there is always an appeal for ascent or progress. Thus a homeless guy will look for a roof, the one who has a roof will look to improve the household, or find better accommodation, and then he may look for an extra country house or for a better house and so on. The community on the other hand may take care to improve the roads, the school, the public buildings, the hospital, the port if any, the museum, the stadium and so on.

In this never ending spiral, humans employ vision and commitment to their particular mission. They follow hierarchy and hierarchical order, priorities, tackle emergencies and apply standards to ensure better services and products. Hindrances have never been negligible. Apart from thought and emotions which are closely connected, we also have will. A balance between these three functions is very important. Because some people rely extensively on their thought, others are highly sentimental, and last but not least we have men or women of will, with low thought or emotional background. The expression of will is very important in communication with others when people transmit and receive thoughts from others.

By expressing our will we come to an understanding, which may be agreement or disagreement. We express our will by written or oral words or by any other external behaviour which have a meaning, for example, a nod or movement of the hands or the head which may signify yes or no. An expression of will may be explicit or implicit. When the content of the expression is one and the same with that of the will, we have agreement between the expression and the will. When the content of the expression is not identical with the content of the will, we have dissension. A dissension may be voluntary in the case of a joke or of simulation. Such expressions are invalid and are not binding.

A dissension may be involuntary in the case of error. Such error occurs when the knowledge on which an expression is based is wrong or when an expression is based on ignorance. An error may be due to a variety of reasons. When an error is important an agreement is not invalid, but can be annulled. Such error may concern the person, the thing, the kind, the amount, the place or the time involved. Error and a probable inconsiderate initiative may frustrate the course of an action or the expected outcome. Second thoughts are inevitable; reconsideration of the data is a must as well as the taking of corrective action.

24
Daily Practice

However, it is necessary, as we have said before, to practise this technique daily; there is great strength in repetition.

You can use visualisation in whichever sector of your life and for whatever achievement you would like to accomplish. You see, you are not infringed by reality. You are restricted only by your own capacity to master your thoughts.

When exercised properly, visualisation affects and guides the universe to bring to you the exact situations and conditions that you wish for. You can call it magical, superb, spiritual, whatever you like.

Remember and understand clearly, that whatever thought you put and retain in your mind will produce an outcome.

Your power to think thoughts is the power that enables you to create your life, and to make the changes that you wish to happen in your life. Once you understand how to develop it and how to create instead of reacting, this is the greatest and most precious power that you have.

"Concentrate on the ideals which you desire to see manifested in your life."
Charles F. Haanel, *The Master Key System*

Will Free from Defects

In both instances of voluntary or involuntary dissension, true will is absent because of the dissension between the will and the expression. In other cases, as in the case of fraud or threat, though true will exists, this "will" may be defective because the motive that produced the expression is reprehensible. Fraud is

84

an illicit misleading of a certain person. Every intended conduct having a tendency to produce, strengthen or maintain an erroneous perception or impression falls within the context of fraud. Such conduct may be founded on false pretences, concealing or hushing up or imperfect communication of the facts.

In fraud we do not examine if the error brought about is material or immaterial, pardonable or unpardonable. What counts is the intention of the swindler to bring about the defective expression of the will of the deceived. The deceived seek the protection of the court and claim the annulment of the defective action or claim damages. Fraud is a civil wrong, as well as an offence in criminal law. Threat is another defect of a person's will. A threat may be absolute as in the case of bodily force, or may be compulsive as in the case of psychological force. In the case of absolute force, we do not have defective will, because no will is expressed and consequently there is no action. An agreement which is the outcome of absolute force is null and void, while a compulsive agreement is liable to annulment before a competent civil court. The precepts for such annulment are:

1. The threat exposes a serious and immediate danger to life, bodily integrity, freedom, the esteem or the property of the person or of the next to kin of the person threatened.

2. It must be such that objectively viewed causes fear to a person of sound mind, that is a person of good sense, having the ability to discriminate what is a serious and what is a vain fear.

3. It must be against a person engaging in some kind of business and the threatened ill must be under the power of the threatening person.

4. It must aim at the concluding of a contract and indeed the concluded contract must have resulted from the threatened fear.

5. Such threat must be contrary to the law and or proper morals.

25
Choose a Quality You Like

Choose one quality, one value or one talent that you would like to improve and would desire to possess, such as:

- Being more diligent;
- Being more compassionate;
- Being more lovable;
- Being more organised;
- Being more serene;
- Having better self-confidence.

Visualise this quality for five minutes every day.

Also practice seeding. Implant the feeling you are the person that you would like to be. Connect with this emotion and appreciate how you feel being that person. Determine you are organised, diligent, calm, self-possessed and confident of success. Have all your attention centred on this particular quality, going far like a person of deep insight. Practice this technique five minutes every day, have that feeling and believe it.

"Skill gave rise to chance and chance to skill."
Aristotle *Eth. Nic. VI.* 4.

The Autonomy of the Private Will

The true and valid expression of our will is subject to safeguards by the law and legal order. As a rule, most agreements and binding contracts are informal. This rule facilitates every day transactions, while formality makes transactions harder. Formality is safeguarded by the use of records and documents. In our days, the information technology facilitates to a great extent the keeping of records and the carrying out of transactions not only at a much more efficient pace, but also within remote geographical destinations. Formality stops a person from acting hastily; it helps from the earmarking at the preliminary negotiation stage to the final conducting of the contract; it protects third parties and facilitates the proof about the existence or non-existence of a contract.

When formality is agreed by the parties, non-observance leads to invalidity, except when the parties being aware of the omission fulfil the contract. When a formality is prescribed by law, non-adherence leads to invalidity, except when a different consequence is provided. In the former case, formality is a component part of an agreement, because the agreement does not exist without the required formality. A formality prescribed by law is essential not only when an agreement is concluded, but also when amendments take place. The principle of the autonomy of the private will is recognised in most jurisdictions and is of foremost importance in transactions and has contributed greatly to the progress of the economy. On the basis of the autonomy of the private will, people are the law makers of their own relationships.

In most jurisdictions, an agreement contrary to a forbidding provision of the law is invalid. The same applies to agreements contrary to proper morals. A contract is required by law for the conclusion or for the varying of an obligation.

A right cannot exist without a duty based on our sentiment of liberty and on the conscience of a free umpire who oversees our decisions and free acts. A right and a duty put together are the two components of justice. The twofold character of justice corresponds to these two components and gives rise to the *claimable* and to the *compulsory*.

Creating our life and making the changes that we wish to happen in our life relies on the exercise of our formative rights within the context of the *claimable* component. On the other hand, the *compulsory* or *coercive* component entitles us to the protection of our life, liberty and property, being a triad of absolute rights, through *due process.*

26

Master the Six Laws

Take the Six Laws of the Power of Thought and of the Mind and copy them in a personal manner, such as:

- My thoughts are real powers.
- My mind is a transmitter and receiver, broadcasting and receiving thoughts.
- The thoughts that I think with emotion have a magnetism that attracts the desired outcomes to me.
- I always think thoughts, but I have the ability to retain a certain thought or dismiss it.
- I have the power and the ability to put in my mind any thought that I like.
- My internal world and my external world are connected.

Once more, for five minutes every day, have in view as a purpose, intention or possibility your deep interest in the effectiveness of the Six Laws in your life. Consider their effect. Wonder how they operate and bring about the intended results in your life. Practise the technique of contemplation that is not superficial, but with more analytical thought, extending beyond the surface.

"Thought is the fire that creates the steam that turns the wheel of fortune."
Charles F. Haanel, *The Master Key System*

Synergy

By relating the techniques proposed in previous Chapters 7 and 21–26 to an upgraded level we enhance our autonomy of private will. In due course, we can bring about the desired results in our external reality. At the starting point, we had in mind a set of targets we wanted to achieve with regard to our earning position, health, exercise of a new job or trade, or to our personal happiness. With the techniques proposed in the preceding chapters we were able to acquire a mind control shield from external undue influences and establish our own guidelines and strategy on a more advanced background.

We have already enriched our predominant mental attitude through new experiences and have streamlined new qualities that we have included in our pursuit for better results. Our intelligence, wisdom and aptitude for the creative arts are on our side. Our mind is the seat of our intellectual abilities that enable us to perform mental activities which in their turn were taken into consideration for college admission or for job performance in organisations. Such abilities include numerical aptitude, verbal comprehension, perception, inductive and deductive reasoning, spatial visualisation and memory.

Our bodily formation and physical abilities are also required in jobs in which success requires stamina, dexterity, and other similar characteristics. Both our mind as well as our body can adapt to required standards through learning. This aptitude of the human mind and body is shown in the motto, "I get older being taught a lot at all times."*[3]

Learning in this sense is defined as a change in behaviour that occurs through experience. Again, by being taught we develop our power of thought to include new usages in our ability to perform new tasks either mental or physical. Synergy

---

[3] *Γηράσκω δ'αιεί πολλά διδασκόμενος. Solon. Law maker, elegy poet, one of the 7 wise men.

comes about as a reward to those who enjoy the discovery of new venues and possibilities.

Undoubtedly, synergy in this sector is highly complex and outside the perception of many persons. Also the risk of failure or setbacks is omnipotent having a discouraging effect. A synergy of so many factors as we have seen in the previous chapters requires an element of a high degree of perseverance, optimism and even sometimes some degree of good fortune. Fortunately, attitudes to learning have improved considerably in the latter half of the last century and in the present era encouraging and enlarging the scope of adding new or improving old qualities we deem essential for our success. What remains is a habit to plan ahead, to review and evaluate our progress on a regular basis.

27

The Tongue of the Universe

Write in your personal diary the following statement: The power of thought is to think thoughts independently and beyond real circumstances around me.

I want you to think in depth, contemplate, for five minutes every night this statement: "I have the ability to think whatever thoughts I desire."

I want you to clearly realise that the power of thought is not to react to circumstances and situations. The power of thought is not to see what is happening in your life. The power of thought is to intervene and create something that does not yet exist.

The power of thought is to penetrate your internal world and to create the conditions and circumstances you wish, and to acquire, live and feel the satisfaction that you possess this mechanism; this is the tongue of the universe. These are the vibrations, the pulses of the universe. Everything in the universe is made up of vibrations and you are a possessor of this mechanism that produces these vibrations. You can penetrate this mechanism, by putting any thought you desire in your mind.

> **"And mind, which flows through the whole mass (of the universe) mingles with that vast body."**
> **Æn. VI. 726.**

Independent Thoughts

Thinking thoughts independent from data looks a very randomly and untenable allegation. For how can one cross a bridge without arriving at the crossing, near the road, or river? This is very odd, at least when one contemplates any future happening. However, when we think in retrospect, we have an infinite number of examples.

Then you may happen to see two people working hard in the open air. The one digs a hole, and the other pushes the soil back into the hole. Amazed with their activity, you go near them and ask them about their job. The one who digs the holes looks up and explains to you: "My job," he says, "is to dig the holes. My friend's job is to push the soil back into the hole."

"You see," the other man explains, "we were three. We had with us another guy whose job was to plant the tree."

"Really?" you exclaim. "And what happened to him?" you ask.

"You see, we had budget cuts," explains the digger. "The posts were reduced from three to two; so now we are left with only us two getting on with our jobs."

These two guys certainly think thoughts independent from reality. Once they go on doing their job and get their pay, why bother about other issues? Anyhow, this option seems to be based on a fallacy. One might call it bad or one of the worst. Tax payers, stakeholders or the auditors will sooner or later get the queue and frown at them.

There are other options that would not be as bad. For example, plant a smaller number of trees, reduce the job to two thirds so as to keep the three working on, on the project. There are still better options. If they get a faster digging device they become more efficient, or they could assign the planting to a voluntary organisation, when the project is for the community where the community can undertake only the basic expenditure, or even find a sponsor to help. Causality and purpose are very important instruments in moving people towards action. There is always a "Why?" question to ask and a "For what purpose?" And then economists ask three well-known questions, "What to produce, how and for whom?" All the knowledge and wisdom of economics starts from these three basic questions.

Besides the six good servants that are able to help you in diagnosing a real situation, you have also the assistance of logical arguments that can help you check whether a given situation conforms to prescribed norms.

28

Self-Awareness

Practice self-awareness. Ask yourself two questions many times every day:

First question: How do I feel?
Second question: What do I think?

Next, uproot any negative thoughts. Practise these techniques. Choose whichever technique you prefer. In short, begin to cultivate your mind. Practise these exercises. There is a great difference between simply thinking thoughts and working with the power of thought, in a tactical and organised method.

The difference between the former two is like the difference between theory and experience; and most of all, it is the difference between failure and success. For this reason, you can understand that from now on, the most important part of this technique will be the time that exists between each exercise.

"Character is not a thing of chance, but it is the result of continued effort."
Charles F. Haanel, *The Master Key System*

Right and Duty

The idea of right is connected in an inseparable manner with the idea of duty. The one cannot exist without the other. Duty has been defined as to that which is done with consistency, sincerity and conscientiousness.

Consistency means the keeping of our word (our promises). This virtue comprises self-criticism, self-control, self-respect and self-possession. Consistent persons can confront any circumstances and situations in their life with responsibility and sensibility. Also, this person promotes co-operation with others, mutual respect and the avoidance of telling lies and being a hypocrite. Responsibility prevails in a consistent person's actions, not fear of sanctions. The benefit of consistency is internal calmness and serenity as well as avoidance of distress and anxiety.

Sincerity is a virtue related to harmony and honesty. A sincere person tells the truth in a direct manner. Sincerity is a step towards the command, "Know Thyself." As a divine reflection it reveals to us that which we are in reality and clears the image we have for our own self and from outside influences. Before becoming sincere towards others, one must be sincere to himself. Sincerity comprises uprightness and integrity of character. Uprightness is a fundamental virtue of social life, secures good faith and transparency of intentions. It is also essential in political life securing outspokenness, frankness and responsibility.

Uprightness and sincerity define substantially the quality of dialogue, while insincerity leads to false impressions, cheating, sterile opposition and faulty argumentation. Another part of sincerity is simplicity. Simplicity is the ability to see things simply, directly and clearly,

A conscientious person is one who is guided by his or her sense of duty. Conscientious actions are those done carefully and honestly. Besides conscientiousness, consciousness is also relevant to the sense of duty. A conscious person is awake, aware, and sentient and has knowledge by using bodily senses and mental powers. Consciousness is a state in which a person is. It has been examined in relation to language, computers, robots and artificial intelligence, psychology and medicine. Awareness improves by way of cultivating our mind. Moreover, it gives us a lead against any negative current that comes our way in moments when we are called to stand up for our right to create our life and not to react.

29
Take Control

Every time you think a thought consciously and intently, for something that has not happened yet, you take control and create your life. There are only two possibilities:

- You either create your life, or you simply let it go on by itself.

The second, letting life go on by itself, is easy. It does not need any work; it does not require any discipline. You do not need to use your power of thought.

In contrast, to create your life requires work and discipline. Moreover, by creating your life, you attract power, happiness, success and ability to succeed in your goals. However, if you'd like to create your life you need effort and work. Therefore, pay attention to the way you think every day. What you can achieve is to begin to create with your thoughts and not to react.

Transcend the stage of analysing and agreeing with reality; instead create reality using your power of thought.

"If you wish to eliminate lack, concentrate on abundance."
Charles F. Haanel, *The Master Key System*

Discipline

Discipline is obedience to an authority, or to principles coming from a branch of knowledge or subject of instruction. Discipline usually comes from training, especially of the mind and character, and leads to self-control or self-discipline without needing the constant supervision of others all the time.

It is part of education in schools and of training in military services. It is also maintained by many institutions as part of the keeping of their standards of conduct. The degree of discipline varies, from strict maintenance and austerity at the highest degree to more lenient or equitable standards. Disobedience to disciplinary rules leads to punishment. Depending on the severity of disobedience a member can be expelled from the group, or be subject to deprivation from all or certain rights for a fixed period of time such as attendance, salary or increment cuts in the case of employees or the deprivation of practicing in the case of professional organisations.

Discipline in a way means also exercising authority by persuasion, not by any other means. It relates to the setting of standards and of quality control and is governed by a set of rules. A rule comprises, *first*, the observing, considering or measuring of real facts such as colour, size, length, duration, value and others, *second*, the evaluating of attitude, such as malevolent or negligent and *third,* the setting of quality requirements. The latter are set by the parties in contracts of exchange or by the founders in contracts of association and also by legal provisions.

Albert Einstein expressed the view that, "Respect to authority without thought is the greatest enemy of truth." Such is the importance of thought in matters of discipline. The ability to obey is crucial for those aspiring to exercise authority, according to Seneca, who coined the motto, "He who cannot obey cannot exercise authority." Moreover, Jim Ron, a renowned modern thinker, points out the importance of discipline in the pursuing of targets, saying that, "Discipline is the bridge between the target and the achievement of the target." His advice on discipline is unreserved and straightforward: for every disciplined effort, there is a multiple reward.

Beyond discipline there is of course devotion. Thus Luciano Pavarotti, commenting on his great performances, once said, "Many people think I am disciplined; but this is not discipline, it is devotion. There is a great difference between discipline and devotion." Devotion is a highest form of attachment and ardent love, including zeal and loyalty.

30

Creativity

There are four stages you are going to pass through, when working with your power of thought.

First stage: Sow the seed. The seed at this stage is in the soil; for this reason you do not see any outcome.

Second stage: The seed begins to germinate; but still you do not see any outcome with the naked eye, as the seed is still in the ground. What happens, nevertheless, is that you begin to sense that something has started happening. You are the owner of a right of expectation, of a future prospect.

Third stage: Growth begins to appear and you begin to see some results. Still these are not exactly as you would like them to be but they are beginning to exist.

Fourth stage: Growth is strong and the specific bloom or fruit is visible. You acquire, in other words, the circumstances you contemplated.

"We reap what we sow."
Charles F. Haanel, *The Master Key System*

Nature

We have seen in the quote in Chapter 21 the divine source the being of seeds. Each species of plant or animal, includi human beings, follows its own code or DNA derived from nature. The finiteness of human life cannot aspire to much life of a seed which in many cases gives rise to centena trees, some of which are known to be extant for centuries have an age extending up to fifteen centuries.

Charles Dickens appreciates this parallelism in the opening of his book *The Tale of Two Cities* where he sees the guillotine that beheaded Marie Antoinette as a tree evolved from what once had been a seed in the forest.

Human affairs unravel in their own sequence and order amid historical settings to which we pay little attention in our everyday lives as we are busy with our own priorities and hardly care to examine them in any detail. Though many human beings, like centenarian trees, manage to remain indelible from human memory. Our pursuit in this book is much more mundane and humbler compared to eternity. One such example is an Orphic hymn that extols the greatness of nature and combines her blessings with the wellbeing of the verse composer: "*And to me first of all my soul may in the right road to tread, on the edge of my tongue that never utters a lie Next the tarsus and joints of my body members may be harmless in the measure of this life.*"*[4]

Nature comprises everything that is physical, not artificial; though now we have genetically modified products which seem to be neither natural nor artificial. A naturalist is a person who studies plants, animals and minerals. The information and knowledge compiled by naturalists is indeed vast and valuable from a utilitarian point of view. Let us take *eucalyptus* as an example. This tree grows fast and is particularly popular. Its leaves are used in pharmaceutics, its wood is used for furniture and in buildings. Its bark is used in tanning, in paper making and in the making of ropes. Its leaves and flowers have antiseptic qualities for the lungs, soothing for coughing and bronchitis, pneumonia, laryngitis and pharyngitis. They have expectorant, qualities beneficial for asthma, flu and tuberculosis.

Under this rubric we find a wide variety of creative uses that gives food for thought and for inspiration to many producers. At any given time, we may be users of such products whether their use is brought to our knowledge or is not. They

---

[4] *Anonymous poet. Anthology of Ancient Greek Hymns.

acquire value when in one way or another our life, health, wellbeing or good taste requires them or whenever a relevant need arises.

31
Decision Making

There are three indispensable skills you need to develop to successfully operate your power of thought. (These are decision making, action and persistence, which we discuss in this and in the following two chapters.)
<u>First skill</u>: *Decision making:*

- Know what you want. You need to know what you want before you lay hands on it. This is very simple, but at the same time, very important.
- Be decisive. Say this is what I want to achieve. This is what I want to happen to me. This is the person I want to be.
- On the contrary, being indecisive means you cannot make up your mind; you are not sure or positive.
- Make up your mind. Don't be vague or obscure. You need to understand precisely what you want. Make a decision and say "this is what I want to happen to me, or this is what I want to achieve."
- Your power of thought cannot respond before you know and can clearly see the particular outcome you wish to reach.

"The result of harmonious mental attitude is harmonious conditions in life."
Charles F. Haanel, *The Master Key System*

The Nest Egg

Thinking of creativity in a practical way, we may start reciting an endless list of creative arts and activities. Thus, let us say we have: accounting, acting, baking, building, catering, cooking, cleaning, dancing, diving, driving, embroidering, engineering, farming, gardening, knitting, mining, modelling, nursing, painting, plumbing, teaching, sailing, sewing, singing, weaving. They demand a great deal of sweat and bodily labour as well as planning and co-ordination. In many respects, such activities are interdependent either directly or indirectly.

In the case of Gregg, however, we had a highly imaginative and energetic fellow. His vision was to turn a nest egg project into a great success. His mind was becoming keen on organic eggs. He popped this idea very often into his conversation. Nobody paid attention to him. It was just an idea; but watch carefully what happened to him. He started spending his few savings on fencing and then made a makeshift shed for chicken.

Cousin Seymour gave him a hand in his work. "Hm!" he mumbled. Foxes will kill the chicken overnight. Gregg hardly ate or drank anything then on November 1ᵗ he came up with a thousand chicken, two foxhounds to guard them against foxes and a ton of organic corn. His dream began to take shape.

The testing authority, in their turn, did not favour his project. They dismissed the corn as non-organic. The first test was lost. Gregg would now have to be patient until next June, when new organic grain would be available, upon order and advance payment. Then, the authority demanded the keeping of records and registers. They also prescribed a properly air-conditioned room for the summer months to keep eggs at the right temperature, sorting and packaging equipment, a duly air-conditioned vehicle for distribution to the market as well as regular testing by an authorised vet for chicken flu. Gregg found the first year to be running at a loss, since he could not sell his eggs at the price he expected.

Having no more funds to spend at that time he came up with an agreement with Gerald Dagger, a farm three miles away, to allow him to use their facilities. Egger, his farm assistant, would take the eggs every day for sorting and packaging. Gregg made also an agreement with Moses Jackson for the distribution of the eggs.

To Egger's horror, Gerald Dagger was absolutely hostile to Moses Jackson and especially to his van driver entering his farm. Cousin Seymour insisted Egger should collect the eggs every hour in the summer months, but Egger did not bother about this rule. He collected the eggs at two o'clock every day. In due course, some eggs became stale. That was the end of the egg venture. Angry housewives protested to the stores who returned the eggs back to Moses Jackson.

32
Action

<u>Second skill</u>: *Action.* All your dreams, all your hopes, all your ambitions and your targets will not be forthcoming and of no use, unless you take action. Action embalms the activities we have already talked about. It is necessary to apply them.

- Whatever seed you sow, it is going to produce accordingly.
- Beyond philosophy and beyond understanding the theory, taking action is absolutely essential. Begin doing the exercises and apply the techniques prescribed in this book.
- There is a tiny secret in these techniques. Every beginning is half an outcome. When you start practising, you will find out that very soon you will reach the point you wish for.
- Do not procrastinate. Never postpone doing the exercises. It takes only ten to twenty minutes every day to do them.
- Human beings are by nature sometimes lazy. Defy this rule of laziness. Become diligent and active in order to get from life what you desire. Take action in order to achieve what you want.

"The result of action and interaction is cause and effect."
Charles F. Haanel, *The Master Key System*

Venture

Moses Jackson refused to go on with the contract and Gregg's venture came to a ruinous end. Gregg had to face the worst when the authority stepped in with a criminal charge against him. His only refuge was to dispose of the remainder of 750 chickens and dismantle the chicken shed.

Coming to the keeping of records, Gregg managed as well as he could. Rule one was count your eggs. Every day he was expected to enter into a Register of Daily Egg Production at least two egg collections, the total number of eggs, foodstuff, dead chickens – if any, non-viable chickens – if any, and remarks. Rule two was keep records as regards starting date, age, number, variety, and egg-laying starting date. The third rule was keep a register of daily packaging per egg size, XL, L, M and S by lot of 12 and 30. Rule 4 was to record chicken deaths from the starting date until the egg-laying starting date. Rule 5 was to record the sales per weekday for each client.

Besides all this, a foxhound may turn into chicken eater, and may have to be put down like Gregg had to do with one of his hounds. With all these in mind, a Nest Egg plan may be viable with careful planning, but most important by paying attention to all the daily tasks and requirements, going through the decision making and action stages.

Moreover, getting expert advice is most helpful as well as attending seminars, meetings, and participating in exhibitions, fairs and innovation initiatives. A poultry career is even more rewarding for one opting to engage seriously in a poultry project. Even an MBA qualification may be highly relevant nowadays. Very often you see young farmers attending MBA courses from all the animal breeding range of enterprises, pigs, sheep, goats, cows, ostrich, bees and others.

A fair knowledge on the utility aspects of each industry is vital. From the utility point of view an egg scores high as a commodity. Its protein, known as keratin, provides the building blocks for growing strong hair and nails; and not only that. Chickens fed with green vegetation produce eggs rich in iron or fed with grains rich in Ω_3 (Omega three) produce eggs rich in such oligo-elements.

A venture implies an undertaking in which there is risk. However, having a definite aim and a good organisation eliminates accidents of chance. As you can see even by a cursory look at your local store shelves, good quality eggs are available at competitive prices. Persistence for excellence is a highly valued secret. An overall feasibility study by an expert as well as a good business plan can be good starters, while a careful and prudent implementation matched with an innovative approach are absolutely necessary follow ups.

33

Persistence

Third skill: *Persistence:* This is probably the most significant skill to apply in the work of the power of thought. In whatever you believe as having value and whatever the aspiration you are after, you will find there are difficulties and obstacles.

This is something all of us should have in mind, and this is why most people leave things after their first or second failure. Practising with the power of thought is no exception. In order to succeed, you must be persistent. Work with these techniques, even if you do not see an immediate outcome. Persistence is most valuable, especially when you do not see any immediate outcome. It is then that you must persist to practise these techniques every day.

Repetition strengthens the power of thought. Through repetition the magic mental superpower quality you have reveals itself in persistence. If you do not persist, you cannot expect anything. This argument asserts that if you persist, you will get results. There is a price you must pay for the power of thought, and this price is work, so persist in exercising these techniques.

"The spirit of initiative and originality is developed through persistence and continuity of mental effort."
Charles F. Haanel, *The Master Key System*

Excellence

Whatever activity or enterprise we choose to set in motion, we have standard rules and methods which we can follow. In a contemporary entrepreneurial practice, we have thorough methods of production which we should have in mind in order to overcome the difficulties and obstacles which we are bound to be confronted with.

These comprise the planning of products and the procedures necessary for their production; the provision of raw and auxiliary materials, substitutes and spare parts; the production and assembly line; maintenance and repairs; the quality control of products and services; the cost of production; the storing and packaging facilities; the marketing and sales procedures; the financial, accounting and recording management; legal support; customer service; the human resources management; and finally the secretarial and administrative activities.

The products and services need to satisfy the needs, tastes and expectation of clients. As far as products are concerned, we find quality specifications starting after the transition from the Stone Age to the age of metals in the mid-third millennium BC. The client had always a say on quality upon placing an order for the purchase of goods.

Starting a venture and succeeding involves the combination of a number of coefficients summed up to the harmonious number eight corresponding to the eight musical notes, the first cube called symmetry and denoting also justice and equality. The eight coefficients required here are (a) money resources, (b) officers, (c) personnel, (d) motives, (e) materials, (f) market, (g) information technology, (h) equipment.

This enumeration may sound jejune, but provides the complement to the three important skills we have seen following the process of decision making, action and persistence. Persistence acquires validity when it leads to the achievement of objectives and targets; it stays on the lookout for the harmonisation of interdependent processes, better understanding of roles, improving relationships and lessening of friction. And last, but not least it is guided by continuous improvement through measuring and evaluating outcomes. In real life the pursuit of excellence follows an endless spiral of planning, doing, checking and acting as quality and excellence experts suggest.

In this process dynamic thoughts gain momentum, affording to us new rewards and benefits, made possible through our reliance on the six laws of the thought and of the mind; and what is most important they offer us protection from undesirable ills and circumstances.

34

Thoughts and Health

That our thoughts have an impact on our health is well known in modern medicine, establishing that our thoughts and our health are connected. Prolonged worry, pressure and strain can ruin a person's health. Stomach ulcers are one of the most common psychosomatic illnesses.

Look at what happens when you are angry with somebody. You may shout and argue for one or two minutes and then you realise you start to feel a terrible headache. What brought about this headache? Naturally, it was anger. A strong negative emotion changes the circulation of the blood causing terrible side effects.

Is it possible that thoughts work only negatively? The answer is: "Certainly not." Having seen that thoughts can bring about bad temper and illness, we can see by way of logical consequence that thoughts can heal. This differentiation in the power of thought is of particular importance in cancer patients and the way they respond to their predicament.

"If you want to eliminate disease, concentrate on health."
Charles F. Haanel, *The Master Key System*

Trade-offs

We have so far elaborated extensively on health. Under this title, we examine the impact of negative influences, such as stress, strain, worry or anger on our health on the one side, while on the other we take into account our personal attitude towards our perceived threats coming from our environment. In many respects, reverence towards health draws away many individuals from pursuits of wealth, family, office or even a beloved mate. Such is the popularity of health. For its sake and for its favour mortals condescend to many trade-offs.

Our state of health relies on the good function of our bodily organs and systems including mainly our immune system, cardiovascular system, the spine divided into cervical, thoracic and lumbar, bronchi, lungs, liver, stomach, colon, pancreas, thyroid, adrenal glands, kidneys, bladder and prostate for men or uterus and fallopian tubes for women. The functions of these organs and systems have an impact on our psycho-emotional characteristics involving tension of compensatory forces on stress, fatigue, internal emotional strain and signs of nervousness and irritability; and vice versa, our psycho-emotional state has an impact on our health. While without health nobody is said to be happy, happiness in its turn enhances our health.

Our lot and our fortune are highly delicate matters and the task of striking a balance is an absolutely personal choice. What makes a difference is certainly our attitude, and in our personal progress in the realm of developing our power of thought it plays a decisive role. Penetrating into the internal function of our organs and systems enables us to consolidate their repair, layer by layer, and only when we manage to raise their proficiency to the upper range, can we feel like a healthy rose.

The six laws of the thought and of the mind offer us their guidance at any time in the same manner that providence, destiny and good fortune come to our assistance. The guidance of these laws extends much farther than our domain of health. Our safety calls our attention to an endless number of tasks regulating our relationship with the animate and inanimate world surrounding us, as well as our relationships with other human beings.

At any given moment, our ability to make up our mind on trade-offs is invaluable for our overall wellbeing and our safety. Because our reason recognises the essential, our anger listens to our reason and our desire follows not what necessarily seems pleasant but that which is rational.

35

Be the Doctor Within

The most important thing is to recognise that thoughts affect what happens in your body. How you react to illnesses and what and how you can suggest health to yourself makes a great difference. If you wish to promote your health, you can take advantage of the *doctor within* technique, by including it in your daily plan of action:

- Follow this technique for a few minutes each day.
- Take your dynamic thoughts and inundate your body, with thoughts of health.
- Send your powerful thoughts to every cell, every tissue and every blood corpuscle.

Sickness has no chance to survive in your body, when this is permeated with thoughts of life, power and vibrations of health. You can renew your body every day with your thoughts. If you do this, you will hardly ever be sick. Remember **Albert Swaitzer**: *"The true doctor is only the doctor that exists within us."*

"Where there is health there will be no disease."
Charles F. Haanel, *The Master Key System*

The Price of an Ox

Once, a father presented his son to Aristippus (435–356 BC) and recommended him to become a student in his school. When the father heard that Aristippus's fee was five hundred drachmas, he was amazed. He exclaimed, "With such an amount of money, I can buy an ox."

"Buy an ox and then you will have two," replied Aristippus.

In most transactions, as economists advise us, and as every entrepreneur knows, we have opportunity costs. When we allocate our money, time, labour or whatever resources we have at our disposal, we always consider what is the optimum option we have. Learning is not exempt from this unconquerable law of scarcity. A modern, twentieth century definition of learning refers to, "*Any relatively permanent change in behaviour that occurs as a result of experience.*" In our times, parents usually pay a fee for the education of their children, and moreover, students while learning, have no time to engage in some productive activity that might give them an earned income.

Apart from taking money for his teaching, being the first of Socrates disciples to do so, this little known philosopher makes a very clever promotion of his vocation by comparing a person lacking learning with one whose father opted to forgo a whole ox from his possessions for the sake of his son's education. Such attitude to learning varies in terms of time and place and delving into this issue is an extremely specialised matter. Nonetheless, Aristippus's prompt answer gives us a picture of the difference between one uninterested in developing his or her power of thought and another consciously enhancing this faculty.

Whatever our view on his teachings, his views have a bearing on the objectives of trade-offs we are discussing here. What he suggested was that the goal of life was to seek pleasure by adapting circumstances to oneself and by maintaining proper control over both adversity and prosperity. This is a very highbrow view, one might remark, but it sheds plenty of light on the safeguarding of health, implying absence of pain and proceeding further to the mastery of pleasures. While on the other hand we can admire the sharpness of his wits instructing us to adapt circumstances to us and not ourselves to circumstances. This magnanimous view surpasses any *mauvaise rencontre* or evil encounter premonition. To a large extent life is movement between aversion and desire, but at the same time adversity and prosperity are important milestones for the course of this movement.

36

Affirmation

This technique is as equally dynamic and effective as seeding and visualisation. Affirmation is a statement that you repeat to yourself. You affirm an opinion or an idea, or something that you wish to happen to you. That is, you build up a short statement and you repeat it to yourself continually.

For example you must attend a meeting which you know usually confuses and tires you. You want to be full of confidence and serenity. Therefore, you start to say to yourself repeatedly:

"I feel serene, I feel at rest." "I feel serene, I feel at rest." "I feel serene, I feel at rest."

This is affirmation; a statement that you repeat to yourself in a continuous manner. This statement has an immense strength. By repeating it, you begin to create. You begin to send thoughts to this mechanism that controls your temperament or situation at hand in your mind. By affirming a statement to yourself without it yet being required, your mind begins to listen and form an image in accordance with what you say to it, and the universe follows and brings it into reality.

"Hold in mind the condition desired; affirm it as an already existing fact."
Charles F. Haanel, *The Master Key System*

Suggestion and Auto-suggestion

Having in mind the two essential milestones, adversity and prosperity, determined to move forward and relying on the ability to put whatever thought we want into our mind, we get through certain preconditions. The first requirement is to have a clear perception of the real facts. Careful observation and understanding of these facts is absolutely necessary. The second step towards a designated outcome is a practical requirement involving intention and avoidance of shortcomings due to negligence. Whatever happens beyond intention and the duty of carefulness is due to fortune. The third requirement is the need to understand qualitative preconditions. These may be defined individually, but mostly they emanate from society defined by others. The fourth and last precondition relies mostly on subjective criteria, the weighing of which is based on the judgement of ordinary persons.

We have already commented on attitude under Chapter2 and in more detail under Chapter 13. Mental attitude plays a key role as a practical requirement within the second precondition mentioned above. Therefore a higher degree of attention is required in our mind control practice on our day to day occurrences. This can save us from negative impulses that arise from salacious influences from rude, inconsiderate and generally disrespectful behaviour falling within the rubric of evil encounters. A sound background of self-knowledge and self-confidence is invaluable and most helpful.

Throughout our life, our behaviour is moulded through suggestion and auto-suggestion which can either be unsound and harmful, or may be sound and beneficial. In the case of suggestion, our convictions about the world and about ourselves are shaped through the messages we receive from external sources reinforced with the power of repetition. An internalised suggestion may become auto-suggestion. A suggestion having a negative content of sickness, inadequacy and insecurity cannot affect us when we are alert and have the poise to reject it. It can affect us only when we admit or approve its morbid content thus embarking on feelings of anxiety, disillusionment, sickness, melancholy and indulgence in scary reveries or apparitions.

The cheering note on auto-suggestion is that when geared on a positive orbit it enables us to take control of our character and through the techniques we have at our disposal be able to bring about improvements in our life, especially helping us take care of our bodily condition, dominate over our disposition, replace unsuccessful convictions with better ones and adjust our behaviour to match with a new renewed outlook and also with a new image.

37

Feel Great

Let us make an affirmation together, so that you get to know what it is about. This affirmation is: "I feel great." "I feel great." "I feel great." "I feel great." "I feel great."

- Repeat this statement for four to five minutes.
- Be sure that the power is immense; indeed immense. The most important thing is that you can say to yourself whatever you like.
- Always be precise. State something directed to a concrete purpose.
- Every day affirm to yourself health, success and serenity.

What is happening is that reality predominates. The thought of what and who we are stops us. But this is only reality and not the power of thought. You see, you either bring the situations you wish near you, or you keep them far from you with your vibration and pulses. The reason for keeping the situations you wish away is because reality affects you and you are dominated by it. Wishing to work with the power of thought, you must think in a new and different way, differently from other people.

"I can be what I will to be."
Charles F. Haanel, *The Master Key System*

Dramatic High Spots

Counting our blessings gives us a prop of good feeling. Then we also remember to express our gratitude to all those who have contributed to our wellbeing. Our list of gratitude is very important to us and is also an inseparable part of our strengths which we should take care to protect and to extend to the measure of our ability.

Adversity in its turn is bound to show us our weaknesses and to what extent we have allowed adverse consequences to dramatize our life. Weaknesses may be inherent in our culture, especially in our immediate environment, and may be governed by a system of values which is outmoded or incompatible with contemporary circumstances.

A quality of trust, reliability and good faith may sometimes fail us. We are not always able to foresee sinister outcomes which may befall us. Once such outcomes are not irreversible, or have not passed the critical mass point of no return, we can exert our efforts to overcome the hazards and threats that come our way. Dramatic high spots succeed one another in a very slow pattern. Besides, more often, procedures lag behind, prolonging our state of disappointment, desperation and anxiety. Confusing and tiring encounters may have their share in vexing us and spoiling our good temper. Once we do not internalise their ill effects and have available a good rescue line at our disposal, we can overcome this source of threat. We automatically measure what is the worse outcome of such a threat. Once we judge its size and extent, we can switch on our sense of proportion; thus we cannot be carried away and are able to take control of the situation and regain our calmness and peace of mind.

However, in a growing state of successive financial crises prevailing in our contemporary times, we all happen to feel the grip of corruption reaching more and more individuals. Thus threatening effects do not emanate from ill-gotten characters on whom we have no mitigating influence. Such inconvenience nowadays happens to spring from a more insidious source and these are incidents that we happen to witness very often. And that source is no other than friends or colleagues, gaining an advantage over their own friends and sometimes over prospective partners.

Often the victims are entangled in the law of attraction where instead of happiness they find themselves embroiled in bitter disappointment and as if that were not enough they suffer financial losses on top of it. A similar pattern occurs with unwary partners aspiring for success believing they have found the opportunity they were looking for, but instead finding they are confronted with a dismal failure and financial losses.

38

Life Reflection

Life, being a delayed reflection of your thoughts, is affected by reality that may prevent you from forging ahead. If you are facing problems in your life, then you continuously think that your life or your marriage, or your work are not successful, or you worry about your lack of money and in this way you continually absorb this situation. This way of thinking, constantly recreates the same problem. The power of thought is:

- To go beyond reality. Hold the thoughts that you choose and cultivate them; they will produce fruit.
- Opportunities in your life will present themselves.
- Your reality does not change on its own until you begin to create it, and then you become open to opportunities.
- Know what you want to happen in your life; be certain of this something. Make your decision on this concrete thing. Control and guide your thoughts; create the reality you choose.

"What appears without is what had been found within."
Charles F. Haanel, *The Master Key System*

Providence and Destiny

Providence exists and benefits us without any exertion or labour on our behalf on all those aspects of our life for which it foresees and takes care. She is incorporeal in contrast with Destiny which is different. Destiny has her seat and resides in the bodies where her chain of causes and effects is invisible. Under Destiny, the science of mathematics has been discovered. Thus human affairs, especially all those having a corporeal nature are governed by Destiny. Reason makes patent to us that health and disease, happiness and unhappiness are derived from these sources, according to what we deserve.

Destiny accords her benefits to those of us who live in accordance with nature; while when we are brought up with absurd beliefs or when we happen to find ourselves in a state of weakness, she changes her goods to the worse. This change has been compared to changes occurring from the heat and light of the Sun which are generally beneficial, but can be harmful to those suffering from ophthalmia, a disease of the eyes, or from fever, or to those exposing their skin to ultra-red rays, from which they get sunburn. All the incidents that happen to lead to our wellbeing are directed by a certain force called Fortune. We can cite many instances in our life when we were favoured with good luck and reckon them when we count our blessings.

Our thoughts matter within the context of destiny as they are overseeing all the causes and effects that are mirrored in our life reflection, especially within the juncture where our internal world and our external world are connected. This is the power of thought alongside our Destiny. What makes the difference here is virtue and vice. Vicious people do everything for the sake of riches, but the happiness of such people cannot rid them from their vice, while for the happiness of virtuous people, virtue is adequate. Anger and desire are outside the logical part of our soul, but the logical part of our psyche resides on wisdom, courage and prudence while the virtue of the whole psyche is justice. Justice is divided into three parts, as goodness towards the deities, goodness towards the constituted society and honesty towards our fellow men and women.

The latter norm as we have seen in the previous chapter is grossly circumvented within the virtue of friendship annulling our ability to enjoy the benefit of a free soul mate association with other persons based on mutual respect, appreciation, devotion and trust. As society is adjusting to a rather Hobbesian style without other security than our own strength and our own invention, having no place for industry and other conveniences, the kind of thoughts we think have to become even more inventive towards our quest for success.

39

The Key to Success

The key to success is to start making your power of thought a habit. Habits are very interesting as they are manifested in our usual behaviour. Many things we do spring from force of habit.

What kinds of thoughts we allow is of interest to us. Look at the kind of thoughts you think; connect them with people, situations and various events. Reject disastrous ways of thinking that you may have developed. In their place, create new optimum habits for yourself encouraging thoughts that can help you.

Only **you** can develop your mind. Nobody else can do it for you. There is only one way to do this. Practise the power of thought techniques every day. By making this a habit you will have a better chance to succeed in your targets and acquire the conditions in life that you want.

Doing something once or twice is easily forgotten. Repetition and habit let you embody this power in yourself. You acquire a faithful servant and you can succeed better than working alone.

"Our subconscious mind is the seat of the habit."
Charles F. Haanel, *The Master Key System*

Vice and Virtue

When we set out at the beginning of this book to develop our power of thought, we had in mind the best possible pursuits and not any fearsome spiral of events, such as we have seen in the previous chapter, leading the life of man, solitary, poor, nasty, brutish and short, as described by Thomas Hobbes in his *Leviathan*. Overcoming vice had been once considered a great milestone in human civilisation and the conquest of virtue had its due appreciation. Coming back to our own aspirations to forge ahead towards what we consider to be our target of success, we have seen a number of qualities in Chapter 25 and considered practising visualisation, seeding and other techniques for their consolidation. The concept of virtue is a step further in the development of our power of thought precisely because it is based on the belief that human beings either collectively or individually are capable of evolving morally.

Doctrines about virtue vary considerably among cultures and schools of thought and hence in each personal situation we bear this in mind. We also have in mind to keep all the *acquis* while at the same time we strive to move forward. One view expressed by Pletho is that, "Virtue is the habit through which we are good. Certainly, really good is the deity and we humans become good by imitating deity within the bounds humanly possible." Another view put forth by Musonius is that, "Virtue is science not only theoretical, but also practical, like medicine and music." Dignity and the undertaking of responsibility are important parts of virtue.

Science, nevertheless, is the knowledge of consequences, as we have seen in Chapter 16. By understanding consequences we relate to our aims and means in a forethought circle thus bringing to our focus the practical requirements of the question coming to our attention, in the same way that a doctor proceeds to diagnose the illness of the patient he is examining. A diagnosis may be brief or lengthy depending on the seriousness of the disease involved and when his examination is completed, he comes to a conclusion and prescribes the medicine most suitable for the cure of the illness. In a similar manner, a virtuous individual has in mind what is better or worse and draws from his or her dispensary the most appropriate cure, like an expert druggist noting the dosage and timing of the administered medicine.

The likeness of virtue to music is also an unrivalled example, as the training of the voice requires devotion, zeal and loyalty as made abundantly clear in Chapter 29 and as we can realise in every virtuoso excelling in the playing of a musical instrument, paving our way between the key to success and good habits.

40

Good Habits

Dismiss negative and destructive ways of thought. Create new healthy habits from thoughts that can serve you.

- Do you usually anticipate good or bad?
- Do you search for the good points others have, or do you search for weak points?

These are important questions to keep in your mind.
- Do you have a habit of stating something good to yourself every day?
- Do you have positive statements that you repeat every day?
- Do you employ your power of thought to achieve your goals? Or do you wait until circumstances and situations get out of control?

And always remember, a habit is second nature.

"Our subconscious is favourable for us if our habit be wholesome and right."
Charles F. Haanel, *The Master Key System*

Harmony

Harmony is a common feature of music and virtue. In music, harmony is the pleasant combination of notes sounded together using chords. The musical branch of accords comprising the art of musical ladders is called harmony. Music relies on counterpoint, a melody added as an accompaniment to another melody. The art of counterpoint follows fixed musical rules.

Lack of harmony between sounds and notes sounded together is known as discord. Sound in this respect has an impact on the brain and especially on the row, order or a specific train of thought which can be stimulated by a pleasant melody or hampered by cacophony; and, certainly a sound out of tune is dissonance, being a discordant combination of notes, or harsh tone.

As far as we have our musical predilections, we may opt for good taste performances. However, sometimes it may come to our attention the incidence of new habits appearing in some locations, where especially young people expose themselves to prolonged very loud and also very monotonous sounds purported to be music. This kind of exposure is undoubtedly detrimental treatment for the sense of hearing and is also mind stunting and no prudent person would frequent such locations or allow their children to indulge in such strange habits. Mind stunting habits fall within the notion of discord and are opposite to concord. Concord comes from Concordia, a Roman Goddess, who denoted "Common Heart". Concord is particularly essential to team work and co-operation with others, as much as harmony is indispensable for compliance to the rules of nature and the laws of the constituted state. Symmetry and beauty are important parts of harmony, in which by way of axiom, external beauty follows a sacred law of being in harmony with internal beauty.

Universal harmony has been viewed as part of both the patent and the latent world and also the fitting together of counterbalancing forces. Harmony comprises a dynamic equilibrium or normal functioning of the human body, when all the forces within the body hold equally and are in a state of equilibrium, called "homeostasis". One explanation is that the four liquids, blood, yellow gall, black gall and phlegm, corresponding to the heart, the liver the spleen and cerebrum being in harmony safeguard health, while being in disharmony lead to illness.

And the soul is said to reach a state of harmony when its non-logical parts, sentiment and desire, are united with the logical. The latter is in charge of knowledge, whereas sentiment is governed by urge and desire is in charge of emotions.

41

Subconscious or Sixth Sense

Each one of us is a hologram larger than our conscious self. A hologram lies in all the parts of us. In every little particle we find the whole, like biological holograms in nature, like a starfish.

Being a hologram of the universe, you have a universe inside you. This allows you to draw great power to yourself. You can find answers to your problems and difficulties. But you perceive yourself as an isolated unit. By being a part of the universe you are connected to the universe. This means you have free access to the force that exists in the universe.

All the answers you need for all your problems and difficulties can be given only when you pass beyond the conscious level of your mind. There are three good methods to achieve this: seriousness, desire and persistence.

The greatest obstacle to achieving this end is your belief that it is difficult. There are many methods you can employ to make a decision. When nothing comes to your mind, you can rest and retry the next day. With this simple method you can get the information and inspiration you are looking for.

"Our subconscious mind perceives by intuition." Charles F. Haanel, *The Master Key System*

Our Mental Antenna

Being a dormant fold of our conscience, our subconscious most of the time escapes our attention and remains unobserved; though it somehow remains an extensive background in the periphery of our existence. It provides the data bank of universal intellect to which we have access through our mental antenna. What we save in our data bank may be pleasant, neutral or unpleasant, tackled inside through our five senses.

One explanation why a multiple number of people, who see one single object or scene simultaneously, describe it in different ways and express different emotions seems to be due to this subconscious formation. This is most probably due to the fact that they are exposed to different influences, but it is also due to the fifth law that we have seen in Chapter 3, that we have the ability to put whatever thought we want into our mind. Thus different persons accept and retain different thoughts in their mind. Our objective in this book is to refrain from unhealthy habits, such as reckless spending, and from internalising luring advertising which may be misleading or outside our budget or our priorities.

Life events, such as unemployment, illness, death, divorce or marriage may affect our finances and bring before us difficult choices and decisions under conditions of possible fear, hate, stress, selfishness and others. Under such circumstances a certain degree of flexibility is valuable as suddenly we need to readjust our lifestyle or even our goals and targets. Our subconscious being the keeper of our overall literacy including that of finance and computer can support our adaptability and flexibility required to meet new demands and exigencies.

A systematic practice of the techniques proposed in this book gives us the guidance we need and holds our mental antenna in a good stead when we make up our mind on the issues confronting us. Also when we come to the decision making stage, we examine all the data available to us.

Sincerity is crucial when we take decisions. Honesty and sincerity are fundamental virtues of personal and social life. They go hand in hand with simplicity and good faith and ensure the highest possible degree of productivity and efficiency in reaching our goals, and they also shield our self-image and peace of mind.

42

Ways to Reach Decisions

There are many ways in which you can solve a problem or make a decision. Try to solve a problem logically; but then your consciousness is an obstacle.

Try intuition. As intuition surpasses reason, very often intuition agrees with reason; and then there is no obstacle in making a decision. The problem starts when your intuition points out a different direction. And when intuition and reason are face to face, always remember that intuition is safer than reason and that most likely reason will often cheat you.

Intuition is a great endowment, a tool, a capacity to warn you of up-coming dangers, before they happen, and to indicate opportunities that you can exploit. It can give answers to many questions, about your personal affairs, your job or whatever general or particular matter.

Sometimes the idea you were looking for comes to your mind like a lightning and another time like a silent voice. This is the benefit and your reward for cultivating your mind.

"Intuition usually comes in the Silence; great minds seek solitude frequently."
Charles F. Haanel, *The Master Key System*

Insight

What hampers the solving of a problem is lack of clear perception due to the intrusion of many obstacles in between as it happens in the game of the prisoners' dilemma which seems to be mind-boggling, because it resists each and every attempt at a solution. To a certain degree we are individuals affected by many situations involving outcomes which are inferior or not Pareto optimality as the specialists call them. The study of such situations does not fall within the scope of this book, but we should not lose sight of their existence. As we are not omniscient, we do not know which circumstance will occur to us and when or how or where.

However, opting for a lazy person resting without doing anything may not be the best option, despite the saying, "When you see someone taking some rest without doing anything, help him; nobody died from too much rest." The better strategy looks to be on the side of the players having an eye on developing their power of thought because they are more likely to be able to avoid the worse outcomes.

Insight is the power of seeing with the mind into a problem. A person of insight is able to attract a sudden appreciation of the solution to a problem. Becoming a person of insight is a great advantage. Insight is akin to intuition, the latter being the power of the mind to gain immediate understanding of something without conscious reasoning or study.

As children, we seem to be more open to intuition. If we look carefully, we can recollect important decisions that have proved true and realistic despite the contrary suggestions of our elders. As we get older, our intuition seems to weaken and become more elusive, leaving us a derelict prey to the uninformed and obstinate options of others. Checking out the outcomes as calmly and as objectively as possible in due course leaves us with a sense of wonder. Setting straight a former mischief is sometimes irreversible and when reversible is less rewarding and sometimes vain labour. Still our intuition is valuable, especially when we do not have at our disposal all the information necessary for taking a decision.

Decisiveness is a great virtue showing we know what we want and we are able to communicate trustworthiness to others. This happens particularly when we do not have much time at our disposal to check all the data. Occasionally, it may be risky, requiring a sense of courage and magnanimity towards others. Indecisiveness on the other hand is generally understood as a weakness of character, though second thoughts may sometimes prove a better option.

43

Intuition in Your Life

It often happens that while trying to find an answer to a pressing question, your mind comes to a standstill. Only after a second and third trial does it suddenly yield the answer unexpectedly and helps you reach a decision you are searching for.

Some people notice intuition like lightning or a silent voice. By cultivating your mind, you will come to realise this experience. You will find out in time that this inner voice is your best servant and your best friend. Intuition has been compared to the sixth sense.

Stop your mind at the level of the conscious; do not search all the time as this reduces rather than increases your abilities.

Seriousness, desire and persistence are three keys that allow you to communicate with this rare sense. Dispose yourself to seek the information you need, having in mind you are a hologram connected to the universe.

Thought is a true live energy made up of vibrations. It is a creative energy. It is a reality of a different dimension.

"By keeping the thought in the mind it will gradually take a tangible form."
Charles F. Haanel, *The Master Key System*

Ingenuity

A genius is a person with very great and exceptional capacity of the mind endowed with imagination. Persons of genius have the capacity to be creative and inventive. Genius is also the guardian spirit of a person, place or institution. An ingenious person is one who is clever and skilful at making or inventing, implying the possession of an ingenious mind and the merit of ingenuity made patent by originality in design. Ingenuity is to a great extent a talent transcending intuition as the latter is a feeling manifested in the making of choices. Ingenuity may improve through learning and relies extensively on practice, observation and other related techniques. One important requirement in all fields of art depending on ingenuity is systematic practice and devotion as we have seen in Chapter 29.

Beyond the realm of art, there is also a considerable niche of persons blessed with rare capabilities of perspicacity, showing quickness in judging and in understanding, and keen sight able to look far ahead into what is going to happen in the future excelling and gaining distinction in leadership. As we realise the human mind is extensively versatile possessing, besides other genial influences, mirth, humour and hilarity. Humour is understood as one of certain liquids in the body said to determine a person's mental and physical qualities while hilarity relates to loud laughter, both being part of what is understood as sweet anger.

Leadership itself receives extensive attention in organisational behaviour understood as the ability to influence a group of persons towards the achievement of goals. There is hardly any goal that can be achieved without the co-operation and acting together of a group animated by qualities examined in this chapter and a charismatic leader inspiring courage and enthusiasm. Leadership traits comprise confidence, strong will, determination and decisiveness. To what extent these traits are inborn in some persons and to what extent these persons develop them is an interesting question.

What is certain, however, is that societies are organised around some person or persons in charge or have some head supervising or coordinating their activities. There is hardly any individual goal that can be achieved without accession and participation in an informal group or a highly sophisticated association requiring specific qualifications for their members which in their turn materialise by means of aligning individual abilities and cultivating their minds to match certain standards.

44

The Benefit of Intuition

The benefit of working with intuition is all yours. Thoughts are real powers. Reality does not restrict you; only the quality and quantity of your thoughts, with which you work every day, place limits to your ends. Your thoughts are the particles that make up the circumstances and situations that you wish to happen to you. Therefore, when you start applying the power of thought techniques, you start working with the energy of the universe.

The mind is a transmitter and receiver that transmits and receives these powers. The thoughts that you receive depend upon your own vibrations and their frequency. For example, in the same way that you can turn the knob of a radio or television set in order to listen to a different programme, you can connect yourself with the frequency and the thoughts that you choose. Because when you visualise, you set in motion and start working with the energy of the universe.

If you are anxious you will always receive thoughts of anxiety. Connecting to a person full of self-confidence, you feel self-confidence coming from this person. The vibrations of this person are on the frequency of self-confidence. You can change frequency, by changing your thoughts.

"Your degree of success is determined by the nature of your desire."
Charles F. Haanel, *The Master Key System*

New Achievements

New achievements of human creative activities fall under invention. An invention comprises a rule emanating from the human mind solving a technical problem in a way that was hitherto unknown and exceeds the usual measure of progress. Intellectual products are also the outcome of human inspiration captured by the human mind. The object of a patent, emanating from invention, is the inventing idea by which a certain problem has been resolved.

The intellectual creator can be rewarded in many ways for an intellectual product such as the publication of his or her book, the publication in a periodical, performance or reciting on stage, transmission by radio or television, recording or production on stage or the cinema, etc. In the case of pictorial art the pictures may be exhibited, may be reproduced by copying, photographing, may be included in an album, shown on a screen or be transmitted by other electronic means. The deepest mission of every intellectual product is the communicating with fellow human beings in the present and in the future and the transmitting and diffusing of the meaningful content included in it.

Thus every generation has the privilege to derive a benefit from the support and the source of inspiration of the intellectual proprietor. We have also a number of non-material goods enjoying the protection of the law such as:

(a) the intellectual products of speech and art;
(b) invention leading to patent rights;
(c) trade mark rights;
(d) various other distinguishing characteristics, including names, trade names, and features of shops or industrial businesses and
(e) designs and models.

Generally speaking science, literature, music, pictorial arts, sculpture, theatre, dance, and sports are some of the activities requiring mental creativity on the part of performers and are triggered from the power of thought of persons acting individually and in many respects collectively. Sports events, either in the form of a match or a game or for the purposes of a show, are, as a rule, achievements of bodily skill and strength and not intellectual products. In some exceptional cases a spectacle may assemble the merits of artistic creation, where it is possible to be reckoned as an intellectual product. Sports events attract enormous popularity and collective interest worldwide.

45

Image

Our image is what we believe for ourselves, and the thoughts that we have for ourselves. The way most people think of their image is that it resembles something simple that reflects with precision the person they are.

Our image, however, whether we are looking at ourselves as a likeness or a mental picture, is not static but dynamic. The difference between these two has enormous significance, because you may always agree as to which person you believe and you think you are, and remain in inertia. Or, you may not agree and be on the wing to explore your potential. What you believe for yourself defines who you are. Every person has his or her own "I believe".

The image you have created comes from many situations and circumstances that have happened in your life, which you took and incorporated into yourself. Always remember that you are what you believe you are. What you believe about yourself, based on other people's vibrations is the biggest box in which other people have put you. It's like a cage, or a prison, because, you can never expand outside that image you have formatted.

"Man is the sum total of his own thoughts."
Charles F. Haanel, *The Master Key System*

Cognition

Our personal image portrays our cognitive attributes. It is not surprising that these fall under the scrutiny of cognition, which comprises all the processes that make possible the gaining of knowledge and comprehension and include a whole range of functions: thinking, knowing, remembering, judging, problem solving as well as language, imagination, perception, reasoning, numerical aptitude, and decision making.

Many academic disciplines engage in the study of cognition. Neuroscience, education and logic feature among them and in their turn these give rise to a new field of study known as cognitive science. Cognition relates to abstract concepts. These comprise mind and intelligence and encompass mental functions and mental processes, a synonym for thoughts. Cognition as a term is employed in artificial intelligence. However, only humans have the unique privilege of being able to accumulate knowledge and experience and transfer them incrementally from one generation to another creating human culture.

In general, human beings run their lives by being closely attached to value systems enabling them to regulate their attitude and the processing of information in their minds. Their orientations towards value systems are patently manifested in their outlook and in the goods and services they produce for their own pleasure and profit. These are the outcomes of conversion of raw materials in finished articles or of the performance of skills and arts into services offered. In this perpetual on-going process, individuals strive either singly or collectively to gain competitive advantage over other players or antagonists.

Competition drives producers and performers to add a few advantages, enough to provide potential customers or fans with a feature or innovative idea that gives them a greatest sense of value very often re-inventing their products or services. Thus a great deal of grey matter is allocated in the name of value added to products and services. Many people connect grey matter to intelligence. Persons with unusually high levels of intelligence or unique skills tend to have particularly high levels of grey matter in certain areas of their brain related to their relevant ability. For example great music virtuosi show exceptionally high areas of grey matter in the area of the moving centre of speech which is responsible for the control of the speech muscles.

For those persons aiming to achieve a high standard of performance in their given area of expertise it is essential to aspire to develop their power of thought on the one hand and on the other to endeavour to keep their grey matter in the best possible condition, as this key ingredient of the brain plays an important role in the socio-economic and financial outlook of society. Younger persons are certainly better off in this regard, but with the onset of aging this task becomes harder and requires greater care in order to keep their own image in good stead.

Setting out to earn a living, individuals expect to be rewarded according to the value of products they produce or the value of the services they provide. Their reward is generally speaking regarded to be proportional or in line with the responsibility they undertake and the degree to which their grey matter is able to let them get along with their tasks.

46

Create a New Image

What you can do is to start to recreate your image. How do you do this? You can recreate your image by understanding only one thing, which can convert your whole life. You can become whatever you like once you think of it with continuity. Your image is not a permanent reality for you.

It is from this point that you begin to elevate yourself, when you recognise all your shortcomings, all the restrictions and all your emotions. These are not a permanent truth, but a temporary reality, connected to you only by what you believe about yourself. When you change what you believe about yourself, then your reality changes, to fit with your new elevated image.

The greatest enlightenment will come when you recognise that what you believe about yourself is very small and limited, and what a great superb creature you really are.

Each one of us is a superb creature, because we are unique. Many people make the mistake not to realise this truth, thinking they are ordinary persons, but you must not make this mistake.

"You can be 'what you will to be.'"
Charles F. Haanel, *The Master Key System*

Wit

The concept of wit comprises intelligence, understanding and quickness of mind. Sharpening eyes and wits responds to the demands of sophisticated entrepreneurs. All kinds of games are conducive to this end, while educational institutions never lose sight of this mandate. Wits are in great demand in an emergency, as one must have the wits to realise what to do and act instantly. By having our wits about us we are quick to see what is happening and be alert and ready to act. On the contrary being at our wits' end, we do not know what to do or what to say before a given absurd situation.

Though those having no real background of knowledge and living by their wits, may be clever, but lack honesty being opportunistic. A greatly upset person may be out of his or her wits. Losing control of one's wits implies one is upset and distracted. A similar negative instance occurs when someone drives us out of our wits by behaving in an absurd way. Absurdity itself is part of a logical argument by which the proof of the truth of a proposition takes place by proving that the opposite proposition is false.

Wit is an essential part of all logical arguments, some of which are of great interest in logic. In a contradictory argument, we infer what is allowed or what is forbidden in a particular situation. For example, when entry to a certain place is forbidden at certain hours, by contradiction we infer that entry is allowed during the remaining hours. The silence argument seems to be more complicated in proof, but is very interesting when no distinction is made about a certain category of things or persons. Wit applies also in the other two arguments, the one led from the minor to the major, and the other led from the major to the minor.

Wit is an immediate response to real events at the time they occur. Its performance can vary as we have seen above. It extends to a clever and humorous expression of ideas and liveliness of spirit in conversation and in figures of speech in writing. In all its manifestations, wit denotes the image of the person at a given time. Thus inclination towards a certain mode of witting by habit tends to dominate over a person's image. By applying the technique of self-observation that we have seen in Chapter 5, we can oversee the tendencies occurring to us and be able to handle them.

A good humoured person usually gives the impression of being witty, while in contrast a person lacking wit is thought to be witless or stupid. Thus sharpening our wits gives us a step ahead in developing our power of thought and in improving our image.

47

Your Image is Unique

Not only are you bound to recognise that you are unique, but you must also declare this truth. There is no other person like you. This accords you an enormous advantage when you recognise it. You are also a superb creature, because you are free to do what you want. You can change your profession, if you like. You can move from the town or city where you live now and go to live somewhere else. You can travel to a foreign country. You can learn to speak a foreign language if you decide. You can specialise in whatever trade you like, or hobby, or learn to play a musical instrument.

You have the ability to do whatever you like. You are a unique person and you have immeasurable power at your disposal: your power to think thoughts. Nobody tells you how to think; only you decide.

The law of change prescribes that we become different with the passage of time. Never measure yourself with yesterday's yardstick. Any new information you get changes you. Every positive habit of thought that you learn changes you. You are always in the process of change, and you can succeed, provided you do not confine yourself, holding steadfastly on yesterday's designation of your own, "I believe!" And furthermore provided you always conduct yourself with dignity and self-respect, even when you fail, and also when you succeed.

"Make the Mental Image; make it clear, distinct, perfect; hold it firmly; the ways and means will develop; supply will follow the demand."
Charles F. Haanel, *The Master Key System*

Fascination

Fascination includes both fascinating and being fascinated and comes to us by way of charming or intense attraction. In the latter case, it may occur as if by striking with a thunderbolt as it happens in a *coup de foudre* love or it may not be so sudden, but in any case it works like a dragnet. Fascination triggers off attraction which in its turn stimulates the mind followed by inspiration arousing creative activity in the arts, music, science and literature. Inspiration usually refers to a good thought or idea coming to the mind which may be hope, enthusiasm, confidence or creative power. Looking at events from a retrospective point of view one may evaluate a fascinating occurrence on its own context.

Allure is a tempting form of attraction by posters designed to entice us to join in public events such as concerts, theatre performances or by shop window displays to persuade us to enter the shop and buy goods. Alluring compared to fascinating is rather trickier as it has a higher probability to mislead us or lead us astray from our ordinary course of discipline.

Fancy, on the other hand, is also a mind stimulant to activity which may be chimerical, that is unreal or visionary as in the case of Chimera, a mythological fire-breathing monster, having a head of a lion and a body of a wild goat. A fanciful person is one full of fancies, led by imagination instead of reason and experience because fancy has a real power of creating mental pictures. Unfounded opinions or beliefs or vague ideas fall within the notion of fancy. It extends to things which are not plain or ordinary or to prices of goods unreasonably high or extravagant. An unrealistic fancy of oneself occurs when one has a high opinion of himself or herself, or when one is conceited.

In formulating our own, "I believe" we concentrate on positive habits and reject what tends towards conceit or arrogance. Too much pride in ourselves or in our powers or abilities or too little consideration for others is not helping us in developing our power of thought, or our relationships with others on a solid and secure ground. A similar detriment may occur to us when we pay undue attention to conceited and arrogant persons who have the power to induce us in a wrong direction.

48

Imprinting

To expand our life and our abilities so that we can live happily and successfully, we need to expand our beliefs. This is very difficult to do, but there is one method through the *imprinting* technique, similar to that of affirmation that enables us to imprint new beliefs.

By imprinting a new belief, you take a new idea, and you integrate it with your beliefs. Let us say this idea is that you have infinite power at your disposal. The reason you adhere to this belief is that you have imprinted it in your mind by repeating it to yourself.

The best way to improve your image is through imprinting this notion in your beliefs. This is the new reality of your life. When this becomes a live reality, you have this force at your disposal.

Every morning and every night remind yourself that you have this force. By repeating it you will get up one morning believing that you really possess this great and unrestricted force, and you will realise that you have succeeded in living a more fulfilled life. When this becomes a reality, you can use your new power effectively.

"Our highest happiness will be best attained through our understanding of, and conscious co-operation with natural laws."
Charles F. Haanel, *The Master Key System*

Scepticism

Going through our power of thought we realise a wide range of mind functions and can appreciate how vast is its realm and reach. Thus, when we think, we look, we observe carefully, we can even be speculating or spying on something. We pay attention, we examine, we search or investigate, we take into account, we reflect, we have in our mind, we meditate, we consider, we judge, we conclude, we have an opinion, we provide, we take care, we premeditate, we plan and we also may just have something in mind.

Observing takes place through the senses, while examining is a process followed up through the mind, thought works through a syllogism, it carries out a conjecture, or a reflection. It can also be a continuous concern about what is going to be done about a certain matter or an uneasy, restless or anxious care or concern about a problem, denoted as problematic, when we happen to be in a quandary or cannot reach a decision on a given question.

Scepticism is a knowledge system that denies the possibility of knowing. It also refers to a belief or state of doubt, incredulity or distrust and disbelief, as well as state of pessimism. A fan of scepticism is one who doubts, and is pessimistic on the solution of a certain problem.

Our personal knowledge is the aggregation of learning acquired through up-bringing, education observation and experience. A thorough knowledge on a specific subject is science. In general, we compile and transmit what we know by means of the first law of the thought and of the mind as we have seen in Chapter 3. Omniscience being infinite knowledge is humanly infeasible. Our lifespan, our time and energy do not allow us to expand our knowledge and dexterities to the extent that we might desire, therefore we are usually limited to those fields of knowledge that we consider most essential. Besides, knowledge is useful when it is consistent and orderly classified. A scatter minded collection of information is not of much use.

A scatter-brain on the other hand is one that cannot keep his or her thoughts on one subject for long.

As we have also seen in Chapter 6 that in many respects our conscious mind resembles a very lazy person limiting us to the short cuts available in our environment. Moreover, various centres of power in our society monitor teaching and learning. Inquisitiveness and curiosity do not enjoy much approbation. Though anthropologists, archaeologists and historians find pleasure in peeping into the lifestyles of societies living in remote locations or that had existed in the past. Therefore, scepticism comes to fill the gap in the quest of better answers to existing problems as in those circumstances in which a second thought is better than a preceding one.

49

Undesirable Conditions

Undesirable conditions are those you do not like in life. The way we destroy their strength is first of all to recognise reality and all that is happening in your life. You recognise that all things happening to you are a delayed reflection of your thoughts. These conditions have their causes and their roots in the past. What you must do is:

- Not to react to undesirable conditions and stop feeling self-pity. In the Far East, daily situations are the so called Karma. These are the things that happen to you every day. They have their roots and their causes in the past, and for this reason you do not have any control over them. Still, you have control over the future. You can decide what course of action to follow in the future, depending on how you are thinking now.

- Start creating your power of thought mechanism. Begin to transmit new energy, depending on what you wish to happen to you. Bring the circumstances and situations that you desire near you.

- Refrain your thoughts from undesirable circumstances and situations; thus you take away their strength. It's like cutting the root of a plant and letting it die in a few days, as there is no way for it to be nourished.

"We gain strength in proportion to the effort expended."
Charles F. Haanel, *The Master Key System*

Sagacity

As far as desire is concerned, its objective is to succeed in what we desire, while aversion is to avert what we dislike. Thus, failing to realise what we desire, we are simply unlucky, while failing to avert what we dislike, we become miserable. Navigating between these two important milestones, good luck and happiness, we have our own sagacity to depend on.

Sagacity as a quality endows us with the benefits of nimbleness and versatility of the mind and as a virtue allows us to understand things as they really are and to choose the best among two or more solutions. As a virtue of the mind, sagacity enables us to evaluate and judge correctly a given situation and to find the similarities and analogies among dissimilar things.

This ability is indispensable for taking right and fair decisions. The opposite of sagacity is dull-wittedness and dullness which in extreme cases may amount to a mental disability, while in not-so-obvious cases it may appear in the form of acrisia inanity or coufonoialight-mindedness which we have examined in Chapter 17. Sagacity is not identical with aptitude and quickness for learning, nor the inherent inclination for learning or genius. Moreover, it is not identical with fondness of learning. It is the ability of having a penetrating and impartial critical thought in our everyday life. In a philosophical context, sagacity is the possibility to follow great truths in a comfortable manner. It is also good marksmanship, an ability we require in order to be successful in our goals and in our navigation as we move in between desire and aversion.

From Aristotle's point of view, sagacity plays a very important role in the scientific explanation of things as well as in pinpointing the mean between two extremes without delay, or rather immediately without taking time to think. The stoics view sagacity as subordinate to rationality and prudence together with five other virtues, "good thinking" which is the perfection of thinking, the excellent use of rationality, "good marksmanship" which is the ability to be successful after effective focusing or forethought, sensibility and inventiveness.

Under the Roman tradition, sagacity is viewed as ingenuity, which we have seen in Chapter 43. This is an intellectual talent, having the place of an internal demon. This talent can be substituted through continuous exercising by focusing on a given object which very often proves more effective than sagacity and talent. This approach reminds us of the notion of skill, which we have seen under Chapter 11, and also of the significance of will which we examine in Chapter 50.

50
Will

Will is a very dynamic device, which you can use in the pursuit of the power of thought. Will is both decision and persistence. It decides to do something and persists to accomplish it.

Will does not recognise failure; it is patient. It does not recognise restrictions; it decides and acts. It is creative; it uses all the powers of the mind and teachings of mysticism. Whatever you state with will, shall happen.

Thoughts imprinted with will become very dynamic. Equipped with will, personal strength and personal integrity, you are bound to succeed. An act of will with interest is will with motive, hence an effect with a cause, as much as the opposite, as explained by Schopenhauer, is an effect without a cause.

When will and imagination are face to face, imagination, in the words of Emile Coué, is bound to win.

"You are visualising entity. Imagination is your workshop."
Charles F. Haanel, *The Master Key System*

Personal Power

Undoubtedly, when we come to consider our personal power, we realise that of all the things that exist in the world, we have those which we have under our control and also there are those things which are beyond our control. The former things depend on our actions and omissions, while the latter are lying beyond our will and determination. Though there are no hard and fast borderlines between the two.

When our control increases, we may get more things under our personal power, while when it decreases we lose power. It is generally better to have one bird in our hands, than having one overhead.

Getting overwhelmingly concerned with the ups and downs of life may not be extremely prudent. As soon as we have an unpleasant thought, we have seen the techniques which we can apply in Chapter 14. We simply take it as, "an impression, an unlikely phenomenon." We could still remember to examine whether this idea pertains to those things which are under our control. If so, we have the discretion to do what we deem proper and right. However, when the relevant events are beyond our personal power, we can assure ourselves that these events should not concern us. Attitude, we have also seen, plays a decisive role in many borderline situations especially when we are faced with trade-offs. We have seen both in Chapters 13 and 34 respectively.

Will is however a rational or well-measured desire and is governed by intention and purpose; it also forms an essential part of voluntary acts. Whim is a variation of will as it comes to us as a sudden desire, fanciful idea or wish, often about something unusual, having no rational or well-measured background. Whim is usually a transitory imagination stroke. Too much insistence on whims marks a person out as whimsical, having a different rhythm from others and may be strange; but even whims, whatever their origin or influence, are part of our freedom of thought.

The acknowledged train of thought involves forethought and planning, doing, testing and acting. Without checking and testing, mistakes and errors are bound to occur. An ideal state of faultlessness has been deemed highly unachievable, but behaviour, disposition and actions in serious life matters involve a human sense of responsibility lying within personal freedom, overriding freedom of thought, and the expectation for excellence. We reach excellence by overcoming imperfections. We do this with a light touch, having in mind and mastering the techniques proposed in this book and also appreciating its bountiful richness.

Bibliography

- The Power of Thought, Handouts in Greek Language, By Nicki Michael, Clinical Psychologist.
- Charles F. Haanel, *The Master Key System*.

Testimonials

It was very positive reading for me – I learned a lot from Argyro Toumazou's writing. I am sure she will interest a lot of readers who seek their own truth and wonder how to improve their life but do not have the tools for it.

—Hélène Tzico Stefanesco

I very much enjoyed reading Argyro Toumazou's book – I will definitely work to develop my power of thought!

—Elisabet Myrhed Aiezza